AF316768

VIGOROUS

Overcoming Schizophrenia and Finding Strength Through Faith, Connection, and Self-Acceptance

CONTENTS

ABOUT THE AUTHOR

My name is Nicholas J. Cortez. I come from a Dominican and Puerto Rican background, but I was born and raised in the United States. Growing up, life wasn't always easy. My family was far from perfect—there were struggles, and things didn't always go smoothly. But even through the chaos, I found a way to stay on track. In high school, I made it onto the honor roll while playing sports like football, lacrosse, and track and field. I even got the chance to play Division 2 college football during my first year.

I developed a love for the arts alongside my academic and athletic pursuits. Drawing has always been a passion of mine, and in high school, I became part of the Arts Honor Society. My first job was at a pretzel store, but my interests went beyond that. Over the years, I found myself drawn to nursing, and today, I'm working as a nurse while also studying to become a registered nurse (RN). When I'm not busy with school or work, I spend time on music, another one of my creative outlets. I live for moments of artistic expression through drawing, music, or being in nature.

I wrote "Vigorous" because I believe my story can help others. Living with schizophrenia has been one of the hardest challenges of my life. I've experienced things that most people can't even imagine, from intense paranoia to hallucinations that felt all too real.

But despite everything, I've managed to come out the other side, and I want to share that journey. "Vigorous" isn't just a survival story—it's about finding strength when everything seems hopeless. My goal is to shed light on schizophrenia, a condition that is often misunderstood, and to bring awareness to mental health issues that many people face in silence.

INTRODUCTION

I thought I was going to die.

Not just once but over and over again. Paranoia crept in like a shadow I couldn't shake, gripping me so tight that I lost all sense of reality. I was convinced people were spying on me, that someone had hacked into my phone, and that my neighbor had implanted a chip in me while I slept.

But the worst part? I truly believed that God wanted me to send this man to hell. That was the state of my mind during my darkest days, right before I shot someone and ended up in jail. It wasn't me acting out of anger or revenge—it was schizophrenia taking over my life. It was fear, paranoia, and delusion all rolled into one uncontrollable force.

If you've ever felt like your mind was betraying you, or if you've ever struggled to understand someone who is, then you already know part of what I'm talking about.

This book isn't about me trying to look like the hero of my own story. It's about survival, recovery, and hope—both for myself and for anyone who has ever faced mental illness. I'm writing this to help you understand what it's like to live with schizophrenia. It's not just hearing voices or having strange thoughts; it's a constant battle with your mind.

I also want to bring awareness to the struggles that people with mental health conditions face every day. It's more than just medication and therapy—it's about trying to live a normal life while dealing with an illness that most people don't even begin to understand.

Right now, many people still don't talk about mental health enough. We live in a world where ignoring what you don't understand is easier. The truth is schizophrenia is not something that goes away with a pill. It's a constant journey. And sadly, there are still too many of us battling this illness in silence, unsure of who to turn to or what help is even available.

Society might have come a long way in some areas, but there's still a long way to go in breaking the stigma surrounding mental health. The bad news is that if we don't change how we approach this, more people will continue to suffer in the shadows.

But there's also good news. You don't have to stay in the dark. I didn't, and neither do you. Through prayer, faith, and the help of family and friends, I found a way to manage my schizophrenia and build a life that I can be proud of. I'm here to tell you that there is hope. Life doesn't have to end with a diagnosis—it can get better. The journey is long, and the road is hard, but with the right help and the right mindset, you can make it through.

In this book, I'll walk you through my own story. You'll see the highs and the lows, the moments of pure terror, and the steps I took to come out stronger on the other side. Along the way, I'll share the lessons I learned, the coping strategies that helped me the most, and the steps that might help you or someone you know going through something similar. Whether learning to lean on faith, finding the right support system, or simply understanding that you are not alone in your struggle, this book guides you.

Through "Vigorous," I want to inspire others who face similar struggles. Life may not be easy, but it can get better. My story isn't just for those with schizophrenia; it's for anyone who has ever faced adversity and wondered if things would ever improve. I hope this book provides a sense of hope and the belief that brighter days are always possible, no matter what you're going through.

By the end of "Vigorous," I hope you'll walk away with a deeper understanding of schizophrenia and mental health. More than that, I want you to feel a sense of hope. Whether you're facing this illness yourself or supporting someone who is, know that brighter days are ahead. You can survive this and even thrive beyond it.

So, let's begin this journey together. Stay with me, and I'll show you that there is a way forward.

CHAPTER: 1 MY BATTLE AND TRIUMPH OVER SCHIZOPHRENIA

EARLY YEARS AND ONSET

I was born in America, but my roots trace back to the Dominican Republic and Puerto Rico. Growing up in New York was an experience that shaped me in many ways. My family wasn't perfect—there were a lot of ups and downs. Despite that, I always found a way to keep moving forward. My veteran mom was a big influence on me, and she did her best to raise my younger brother and me, even when things got rough.

The school was one area where I excelled. I did well in my classes and was on the honor roll throughout high school. I wasn't just about academics, though—I was heavily involved in sports. I played football, lacrosse, and track and field. My love for sports eventually led me to play Division 2 college football in my first year. Outside of school and sports, I had a creative side. I loved to draw, which led to joining the Arts Honor Society in high school. My first job was at a pretzel store, but my mind was always on bigger things.

THE BEGINNING OF SCHIZOPHRENIA

Looking back, the early signs of schizophrenia were there, but I didn't recognize them at the time. I started feeling like something was off in high school, but I couldn't put my finger on it. It started as a strange feeling that people were watching me. It wasn't strong enough to make me worry initially, but those thoughts became harder to ignore as time passed.

During my high school years, I got into a lot of fights, which landed me in trouble. The school gave me warnings that I would be sent to a secondary school. But one principal worked with me throughout high school, making sure I graduated from a regular school.

When I entered college, those feelings intensified. I started to distance myself from people, isolating myself more and more. The paranoia grew, and I began to believe that people were out to get me. The worst part was that I didn't understand what was happening to me. I thought I was just stressed from school or maybe not sleeping enough. But the truth was that schizophrenia had started to take hold of my life.

I remember the first real episode vividly. I was convinced that someone had hacked into my phone and watched everything I did. I became obsessed with checking for cameras and figuring out who was after me. It was terrifying, but I didn't know how to explain it to anyone. How do you tell someone you believe people are spying on you through your phone? It didn't make sense, so I kept it to myself. That was the beginning of my long struggle with understanding and coping with schizophrenia. At the time, I didn't realize how much this illness would affect my life. I just knew that something wasn't right.

THE COLLEGE YEARS

Starting college felt like the beginning of something great. I had dreams of getting my degree and making something of myself. I wanted to pursue biology and eventually have a stable career. Even though I didn't live on campus, I was determined to do well. I commuted to class daily, trying to stay focused on my future. It wasn't the typical college experience, but I made it work.

But as the semesters went on, things started to change. I didn't make many friends, and commuting kept me from experiencing the full college life. I slowly began to pull away from the few people I knew. I would tell myself it was easier this way—that I didn't need the distractions. But deep down, I knew something was wrong. The feelings I had in high school were getting stronger. The paranoia crept in, and suddenly, I felt like everyone was watching me. I began to suspect people were plotting against me, trying to cause me harm. I didn't know why, but I couldn't shake the feeling.

I also started smoking weed in high school, and later, in college. I was self-medicating. It began socially, like at parties where I smoked weed and drank alcohol. But over time, I would self-medicate more when I was alone. This made my delusions and hallucinations even worse.

I remember one specific instance in college. I smoked weed before going to the library to study, and when I sat down, I felt like everyone around me was watching me, analyzing everything I did. I got really paranoid and had to leave and go to a different library.

THE DOWNWARD SPIRAL

The more isolated I became, the worse it got. I was constantly on edge, feeling like I had to keep looking over my shoulder. It started with small things, like thinking people were watching me on the bus or keeping tabs on what I was doing in class. But soon, it grew into something much bigger. I began to believe that people could read my mind. It was terrifying, and the fear took over. I couldn't tell anyone because I didn't know how to explain it. So, I just kept quiet and stayed alone.

Even though I was going through all of this, my academics remained my main focus. I didn't let my grades slip and kept working hard to graduate. I still loved music, something that brought me some peace in the middle of all the chaos. But I was living two lives—the one everyone saw, where I was just another student doing my work, and the one inside my head, where I was drowning in fear and confusion.

Socially, I had cut myself off from almost everyone. I stopped contacting old friends and didn't bother making new ones. I couldn't handle the thought of people getting too close, so I kept to myself. The loneliness was overwhelming, but the paranoia made it feel like the only option. My mind was a battlefield, and I didn't know how to fight back.

By the time I graduated, I had achieved my goal of earning my degree, but at a great personal cost. The stress had been building for years, and while I had succeeded in my studies, my mental health was unraveling. I left college with a diploma but a growing sense that something was deeply wrong with me.

THE BREAKING POINT

By my senior year of college, things were falling apart. I was convinced that people were spying on me. Everywhere I went, I felt like I was being watched. I became certain that the Secret Service had hacked my phone, controlling my camera and tracking my every move. The fear became overwhelming, consuming me day and night.

At the time, I lived alone with my dog, who comforted me in all that chaos. But the hallucinations and delusions only got worse after I moved to a new apartment. I started believing that God was watching me constantly, judging everything I did. It wasn't just a religious experience—it was terrifying. I thought my life was coming to an end. I spent hours reading the Bible, convinced I needed to be perfect or face unimaginable consequences. The fear of God's judgment kept me awake at night, spiraling deeper into my delusions.

My mind was a mess, and my apartment started to show it. I believed cameras were everywhere, hidden in the walls, watching me. I taped over every hole to block out these imagined cameras, but the paranoia wouldn't stop. I even convinced myself that my neighbor had broken into my apartment and implanted a chip inside me while I slept. I believed God wanted me to do something about it—to send this person to hell.

One night, around 3 a.m., everything reached a breaking point. I started banging on the window to get my neighbor's attention. The neighbors downstairs came up, yelling at me to stop. In a panic, I grabbed my gun, broke a hole through the door, and told them to back off. They left, and I returned to the window, still trying to get my neighbor to come out. When he finally did, I shot him in the hip.

CONSEQUENCES

The police arrived not long after. I climbed out of my window and waited on the roof, unsure what would happen next. I was terrified they were going to shoot me, so I kept my hands up, hoping to avoid any sudden movements. They eventually arrested me and took me to the station. When they tried to question me, I refused to say anything without a lawyer.

From the station, they sent me to jail, placing me in the mental health unit. The first few days were a blur. Someone watched me constantly, keeping an eye on me 24/7. The delusions didn't stop, though. I started believing that the person in the cell next to me was Jesus, and I began hearing voices. The entire experience felt unreal as if I were stuck in some twisted nightmare.

At one point, I pushed myself so hard that I passed out. When I came to, I had a strange moment of clarity. I remember thinking about life, the human body, and how amazing it was that we were alive. But that brief moment didn't last long. Soon, the confusion and chaos returned, swallowing me up again.

When I was in jail, I ended up getting into a fight. It was two people against me, and I won the fight. What started the fight was one of them said something disrespectful to me, and in jail, you can't take disrespect, or others will start disrespecting you too. So, I fought him. During the fight, his friend hit me in the back of the head. I ended up fighting both of them, and I got them to the ground. That's when the correction officer broke it up.

After a while, they moved me from the mental health unit to the general population. I don't know why they made the switch—maybe they thought I was faking it, that I wasn't sick. My mom kept calling the jail, trying to understand what was happening to me. She was desperate to talk to me, but nothing made sense to either of us then. All I knew was that I was trapped, both mentally and physically, with no clear way out.

Before I got arrested, something happened that changed everything. I remember calling my ex-girlfriend, Sam, from high school. I had always cared about her, and I felt I needed to warn her in my paranoid state. I truly believed people were out to kill both of us, and I didn't want anything to happen to her.

I'm sure I sounded completely irrational, and she was understandably confused. I could hear the uncertainty in her voice as I told her about the danger I thought we were in. She didn't know what to do, but after our call, she contacted my mom and told me what I said.

When my mom heard everything, she lost it. She called me right away, demanding to know my pastor's number. I never imagined things would escalate this way, but that phone call was a turning point. If I hadn't contacted Sam, my mom would have never known how serious my situation had become. She contacted my pastor, who, in turn, connected her with a great lawyer. That lawyer played a huge role in helping me get out of jail.

But before things got better, they got a lot worse. After they moved me to the general population, I started losing control. My paranoia and frustration boiled over, and one day, I ended up spitting on a correctional officer. That wasn't enough for me, though. I challenged him to a fight, daring him to pull me out of the cell. He didn't hesitate. The officer pulled me out, and I swung at him. That was it. Two other cops jumped in immediately, tackling me to the ground and pinning me down.

After that incident, they sent me straight to solitary confinement. The place was known as "the box," it was as horrible as it sounds. The cell was surrounded by plexiglass, cutting me off from any sense of normal human interaction. It was hard to breathe in there, and I felt like the walls were closing in on me. The toilet didn't work, and the water from the sink barely dripped. I was trapped in that cell for four weeks, isolated and unsure of when I'd be let out. Food came sporadically, and the days blurred together, each one feeling longer and more suffocating than the last.

Before this, I had tried to explain what I felt to my mom. I told her about the "Rainbow People," these strange figures I thought were watching me. At first, she didn't take it seriously. But after my call to Sam, she realized I was far gone. She understood that something was seriously wrong, and that's when she stepped in to help.

As for the gun, I had bought it with no harmful intentions. I was planning a casual outing with some friends from church, a simple day at the shooting range. But things never go as planned when paranoia takes over. The gun, which was supposed to be for fun, became part of the chaos that eventually led to my breakdown and arrest. I never saw any of this coming. It all spiraled out of control so fast.

THE ROAD TO RECOVERY

After spending some time in jail, things took another turn. I had refused medication from the beginning, convinced that I didn't need it. But as my behavior grew worse, they decided to transfer me to a mental health institute. It felt like an asylum—cold and distant from everything I knew. The first few days there were tough. I still refused to take any medication, telling myself that I could manage without it. But the doctors and staff were clear: if I continued to refuse treatment, I'd be there a lot longer.

At first, I dug in my heels. I didn't want to rely on medication. The idea of taking pills every day felt like admitting defeat. I believed that I could somehow overcome it on my own. But the more time I spent there, the more I realized that my situation wasn't improving. The hallucinations and paranoia weren't going away, and I began to understand that if I wanted any chance of getting better, I had to try something different.

ACCEPTANCE AND MEDICATION

It wasn't easy, but eventually, I decided to start taking the medication they offered. I figured if it could help me get out of there sooner, I'd try it. And slowly, things began to change. The delusions that had haunted me for so long started to fade. I no longer believed people were spying on me, and the voices I used to hear became quieter. For the first time in a long time, I started to feel a little more like myself.

I stayed at the mental health institute for about six months. During that time, I started to see real progress. I could have clearer conversations with my lawyer and felt more stable for the first time in years. Surprisingly, during that period, my dad reached out to me. We hadn't been closed for a long time, but now he called regularly. My mom and grandmother also stayed in contact, and that support made a huge difference in my recovery. It wasn't just the medication that helped—it was knowing that I wasn't alone in this fight.

As I continued to improve, my legal team and I decided to go for the insanity plea. I started feeling more in control of my thoughts and knew that accepting help had made a difference. After I became more stable, they sent me back to jail, but this time, I was placed in the mental health unit. It wasn't as isolating as before, and I had a clearer path forward.

Eventually, I went to court. After hearing my case, the judge agreed to release me under probation for five years. Though it wasn't officially called probation, there were strict conditions I had to follow: regular drug tests, continuing my medication, and staying in New York for the next five years. It wasn't complete freedom but the beginning of a new chapter. I finally had a chance to rebuild my life, one step at a time.

LIFE AFTER THE INCIDENT

After the insanity plea was accepted and my case was dismissed, I stood at a crossroads. I was free from jail, but the real challenge was ahead—reintegrating into society. It wasn't easy. Life after the incident required me to rebuild everything from scratch, but I knew I had to take it slow. I focused on the basics, taking each day as it came. Therapy became a regular part of my routine. I attended group sessions where I could openly talk about my experiences and connect with others who understood what I had been through. Slowly, I began to feel more grounded.

Overcoming the stigma attached to my past wasn't simple. People tend to judge what they don't understand, and schizophrenia is often misunderstood. Some people saw me as dangerous or broken, but I couldn't let their perceptions define me. With time, I started reconnecting with family and old friends. It was initially awkward—there was hesitation on both sides—but rebuilding relationships became an important part of my healing process. I had to be patient, both with myself and with others.

FINDING PURPOSE

As I worked on piecing my life together, I began searching for a new sense of purpose. Nursing has always been a passion of mine, and I decided to commit to it fully. I returned to school to complete my LPN, and every class brought me closer to the career I wanted. Nursing wasn't just a job for me—it felt like a way to turn my struggles into something positive. I knew that my experiences with mental health could help others, especially those who were going through similar challenges. It gave me a reason to keep moving forward.

My journey also inspired me to become an advocate for mental health. I wanted to show others that recovery was possible, even when it seemed out of reach. Prayer and faith played a big role in my life during this time. I often found comfort in reading the Bible and talking to God. My faith carried me through the darkest moments and still gave me strength when needed.

With the support of my family—especially my mom—I could keep pushing forward. She helped me get disability benefits, which gave me the time and space to rebuild my life without the immediate pressure of finding a job. Her unwavering support kept me going; I couldn't have done it without her. Slowly but surely, I began to feel more like myself again.

CHAPTER 2: UNDERSTANDING SCHIZOPHRENIA

Living with schizophrenia is like navigating an unpredictable storm. It's a battle between what is real and what is not; the lines blur so easily that it can be impossible to tell where reality ends and delusion begins. Each day feels like walking through a maze, trying to find clarity while your mind works against you. It's as if your thoughts get stolen before they can fully form, making it difficult to express yourself. Sometimes, you feel like an observer of your own life, disconnected from the actions you take or the clothes you wear. It's exhausting, and often you feel like you're being watched—constantly under a judgmental eye, unable to escape. The weight of knowing that success seems out of reach, and that failure is looming makes it all the more overwhelming.

What makes schizophrenia even harder to bear is the lack of understanding from others. When people are sick with physical ailments like cancer, they receive sympathy, support, and care. But with schizophrenia, the reactions are different. People are uncomfortable, unsure, and often avoidant. This lack of sympathy is partly because the illness is foreign to most people. It's difficult for someone who hasn't experienced it to imagine what it's like to have your mind turn against you. Schizophrenia feels like madness to others, and that label isolates you even further. It's not a visible disaster like a flood or a growing tumor—it's hidden, unpredictable, and scary to those who don't understand it.

The isolation that comes with schizophrenia doesn't just stem from the illness itself but from the reactions of others. It cuts deep when those closest to you start pulling away, ignoring what you say, or pretending not to notice your behavior. The loneliness intensifies, reminding you that your world is different. People often don't know how to react or what to say, so they stay silent, making the suffering feel even more personal. This lack of connection and support compounds the tragedy of schizophrenia.

Understanding is key to bridging this gap. When family members, friends, and loved ones take the time to learn about schizophrenia, the mystery fades. The person with the illness is no longer seen as "mad" but as someone struggling with a condition that affects how their brain processes reality. This understanding opens the door to sympathy. When we begin to grasp the daily battles of someone with schizophrenia—battles with their senses, emotions, and thoughts—we start to see their experience as one of profound hardship, not madness.

Schizophrenia is a complex and deeply personal experience. No two people live with it in the same way. For some, delusions dominate. For others, it might be a loss of emotional connection or a persistent disorientation. But all these experiences are tied together by how the brain misinterprets the world around it. And as complex as this is, understanding is still possible. Listening to the experiences of those with schizophrenia paying attention to their stories, helps us see the human being beyond the illness. It helps shift the narrative from one of fear to one of compassion and support.

ALTERATIONS OF THE SENSES

For someone living with schizophrenia, the world can become an overwhelming and confusing place, filled with sensory distortions. It's not just a matter of experiencing things differently—it's as if your senses are playing tricks on you, heightening or dulling without any control. Sounds become louder, colors more intense, and everything that was once familiar takes on a strange, almost threatening quality. You might hear things that aren't there or see objects as more vibrant or distorted than they truly are.

One of the most common alterations is heightened hearing. A simple background noise, like the hum of a fan or distant chatter, can feel amplified to the point where it drowns out everything else. You hear things that shouldn't stand out—whispers, clicks, or even a subtle breeze can feel deafening. This heightened sense of hearing can make social interactions difficult, as every small sound competes for attention.

These changes can be both fascinating and terrifying. In some cases, they enhance the beauty of the world around you, almost like living in a dream. But more often than not, they cause confusion and anxiety. The overstimulation of the senses leaves you feeling trapped in a world that doesn't follow the rules of reality.

INABILITY TO INTERPRET AND RESPOND

For people with schizophrenia, one of the biggest challenges is processing and responding to the world around them. Our brains naturally sort through stimuli—sounds, sights, emotions—and help us interpret what's happening, but for someone with schizophrenia, this process can break down. Instead of automatically understanding a sentence or interpreting a situation, everything feels disjointed, like trying to assemble a puzzle with missing pieces.

Imagine someone speaking to you, and you can hear the words, but their meaning slips away before you can grasp it. The delay in understanding might seem like a pause to others, but inside, it's a struggle to understand what's being said. The brain is overworking, trying to string together each word into something coherent, but often, it doesn't happen.

This inability to interpret visual and auditory stimuli can be frustrating. A simple action, like reading a book or watching a movie, becomes a monumental task. The words on the page blur together, the scenes in a movie feel chaotic, and nothing makes sense. Watching TV might turn into staring at moving shapes and colors with no storyline. Social situations feel just as overwhelming—trying to piece together facial expressions and tones of voice becomes a challenge, leading to withdrawal and isolation.

Responding appropriately to stimuli is just as difficult. When someone with schizophrenia tries to respond to a question or a situation, the brain may produce an answer, but it might not fit with what's happening.

Emotions may not align with the moment—someone might laugh at bad news or respond with confusion when asked a simple question. It's as if the brain's internal switchboard is malfunctioning, connecting wires to the wrong responses.

These challenges make daily life exhausting and confusing. Simple tasks become overwhelming, and communication with others feels like trying to speak a language that no longer makes sense. Understanding and patience from those around can make a world of difference, offering support when the mind struggles to connect with reality.

DELUSIONS AND HALLUCINATIONS

Delusions and hallucinations are often the most recognized symptoms of schizophrenia. They are dramatic and captivating, frequently depicted in movies and books as the defining behaviors of "madness." Many people associate schizophrenia with someone talking to themselves or responding to unseen forces. However, it's important to remember that not everyone with schizophrenia experiences these symptoms, and they are not exclusive to this condition. People with other brain diseases can also experience delusions and hallucinations.

Delusions are false beliefs the person holds with complete certainty, even though they aren't based on reality. These beliefs are often rooted in sensory experiences that are misinterpreted. For instance, hearing static on the radio might be taken as a secret message. To someone with schizophrenia, these delusions form part of a logical pattern—only strange to those on the outside. A simple event like missing a bus can spiral into believing someone orchestrated the entire situation against them. To the person experiencing the delusion, this all makes perfect sense.

Hallucinations are another symptom, but instead of misinterpreting real stimuli, the brain creates sensations that aren't there. Auditory hallucinations, such as hearing voices, are the most common in schizophrenia. These voices might be accusatory, insulting, or sometimes comforting. Though the voices aren't real, the person hears them as clearly as any real conversation. It's difficult for others to understand, but for the person with schizophrenia, these voices are a persistent and often distressing part of their reality.

ALTERED SENSE OF SELF

One of the most unsettling aspects of schizophrenia is the altered sense of self. Most people's sense of identity and physical boundaries is so deeply ingrained that it's hard to imagine otherwise. You know where your body ends, and the world begins. You recognize yourself in a mirror or photo without question. But for someone with schizophrenia, this certainty can break down.

People may feel disconnected from their bodies, as if they no longer recognize themselves. One person with schizophrenia described feeling like a "zombie"— disconnected and almost nonexistent. This feeling can extend to physical sensations as well. Someone might look at their hand and feel that it's out of place, an inch to the side of where it should be, or that their fingers have become longer or shorter. Such distortions in body perception can be deeply disorienting.

In extreme cases, a person may even lose the ability to distinguish themselves from others. Thoughts and identities seem to blur together. One patient couldn't tell whether the thoughts in his head were his own or belonged to someone else in the room. This confusion made everyday interactions feel threatening and overwhelming.

Sometimes, the altered sense of self can involve a disconnection from one's body parts, as if they've taken on their own lives. Arms, legs, and even facial features may feel detached, acting independently of the person's intentions. This breakdown of identity can make the world feel strange and unrecognizable, adding to the fear and anxiety that people with schizophrenia often experience.

These changes can also blur the lines between the self and the outside world. For some, it's hard to distinguish where their body ends and the environment begins. One woman recalled feeling like her own bodily functions were merging with the world around her, leaving her confused about what was happening to her and what was happening outside.

The altered sense of self that many people with schizophrenia experience highlights just how profoundly this illness can affect a person's basic understanding of themselves. It adds another layer to the already complex challenges of living with schizophrenia, making it even more important for others to offer empathy and support.

CHANGES IN EMOTIONS

Changes in emotions are a significant aspect of schizophrenia. Often referred to as "affect" by professionals, emotional shifts are one of the most recognizable signs of the illness. In the early stages, emotions can vary greatly. A person may feel overwhelming depression, guilt, fear or experience rapid mood swings. Later on, many people with schizophrenia develop flattened emotions, where they seem unable to express or even feel emotions. This emotional blunting makes it hard for others to connect with them, sometimes leading to increased isolation.

Depression is a common early symptom of schizophrenia, yet it is often overlooked. Many people experience depressive episodes before showing more obvious signs like delusions or hallucinations. Depression might stem from chemical changes in the brain or from the growing awareness of the illness itself. Sadly, untreated depression in schizophrenia can sometimes lead to suicide.

In the initial phases, heightened or fluctuating emotions are not uncommon. A person may feel extreme joy or intense religious experiences, while in the same period, they may also feel overwhelming guilt or fear. This emotional intensity often diminishes as the illness progresses. However, when these intense emotions linger beyond the early stages, it may indicate that schizophrenia isn't the correct diagnosis and that the person might have a different condition, like bipolar disorder.

Some people with schizophrenia also struggle to recognize emotions in others. This difficulty in interpreting emotions can make social interactions and relationships more challenging. Over time, many people with schizophrenia exhibit inappropriate or flattened emotions. They might laugh in sad situations or seem detached when others expect an emotional response. These mismatches between what is felt and how it is expressed are common.

As the illness advances, emotional flattening can deepen, making the person seem emotionless. Though it may appear they are not feeling anything, studies show that many people with schizophrenia still experience emotions internally but struggle to express them outwardly.

CHANGES IN BEHAVIOR

Changes in behavior are often secondary to the core symptoms of schizophrenia. The unusual behaviors observed in those with schizophrenia are frequent responses to the overwhelming sensory and cognitive disruptions happening in their brains. For instance, someone experiencing sensory overload might withdraw and isolate themselves. This withdrawal isn't just a random behavior—it's a coping mechanism to deal with the overstimulation. Similarly, other behaviors can often be understood as rational responses to the challenges they are facing internally.

One of the most common behaviors is withdrawal. People with schizophrenia may remain still and silent for long periods, even in the presence of others. At its most extreme, this can manifest as catatonia, where the person becomes immobile and rigid. Another extreme is mutism, where they stop speaking altogether. These behaviors exist on a spectrum, ranging from subtle withdrawal to complete immobility.

Sometimes, the withdrawal happens because the person is lost in deep thought, disconnected from the world around them. For others, it's a way to manage the flood of sensory input. By slowing down their movements or going completely still, they may be trying to gain some control over the chaos in their minds. Slowed movements and careful actions are attempts to process the world at a manageable pace.

Ritualistic behaviors are also common in schizophrenia. Some individuals may repeat certain actions or movements over and over again. These behaviors might seem bizarre to an outsider, but they often make perfect sense to the person doing them. For instance, someone may engage in repetitive gestures or strange postures to manage intrusive thoughts or feelings. While the behavior may seem odd, it's their way of coping.

Socially inappropriate behavior is another concern, but it's important to understand that much stems from the internal logic of the person's experience. Though rare, some people with schizophrenia may engage in behaviors that can be alarming or socially unacceptable, such as talking loudly to themselves in public or displaying inappropriate actions. Though bewildering to others, these actions often have a rationale behind them based on the person's altered perceptions and beliefs.

Ultimately, the behaviors associated with schizophrenia, no matter how unusual or "crazy" they might appear, usually have an internal logic based on the person's distorted sensory experiences and thinking. When we look at these behaviors through the lens of their condition, we can better understand the reasons behind their actions and, hopefully, approach them with more empathy and patience.

FRIENDSHIP AND SOCIAL SKILLS TRAINING

Friendship is important for everyone, including those with schizophrenia. However, people with schizophrenia often face unique challenges in forming and maintaining friendships due to the symptoms and brain dysfunction associated with their illness.

One young man, for example, found it difficult to reconnect with his social group after his symptoms improved. He said, "I can't make out their words; I don't know what to say. It's just not like it used to be." Another person described how social situations left him lost: "I get lost in the spaces between words in sentences. I can't concentrate, or I get off into thinking about something else." Given these difficulties, it's not surprising that many with schizophrenia respond awkwardly in social settings and eventually withdraw. Research shows that approximately 25 percent of those with schizophrenia are very isolated, 50 percent are moderately isolated, and only 25 percent lead active social lives.

Aside from the brain dysfunction that affects social skills, individuals with schizophrenia must also contend with the stigma surrounding their condition. One older man, returning to the hospital due to the stigma he faced, explained, "I just can't make it out there. Most people out there won't come near me, or they spit at me in the eye. I'm just like a leper in their eyes." The sense of being unwanted or feared by others often leaves people with schizophrenia feeling like they don't belong.

Fortunately, several approaches can help address the need for friendship among individuals with schizophrenia. Self-help groups, for instance, offer a space where people can connect with others who understand what they are going through. The Compeer Program is another option, which pairs volunteers with individuals with mental illnesses. These pairs meet regularly for activities like shopping, movies, or spending time together. Similarly, the Friendship Network in New York offers a dating service for people with schizophrenia or bipolar disorder. These connections can provide much-needed companionship and support, even if not all relationships work perfectly.

Improving social skills is another way to help people with schizophrenia develop friendships. Social skills training programs can be especially helpful, teaching individuals to recognize social cues, read facial expressions, and engage in conversations. One popular program is the UCLA Skills Training Modules, which have been used to train thousands of individuals in basic social skills. Programs like these aim to equip people with the tools they need to interact more comfortably with others, increasing their chances of forming meaningful relationships.

Clubhouses offer another solution to the friendship problem. These community centers, like the well-known Fountain House in New York City, provide a space for people with mental illnesses to socialize, learn, and work. Members of these clubhouses often experience lower rehospitalization rates and greater satisfaction with their lives. Clubhouses focus on creating a supportive environment where members can form lasting friendships while receiving vocational, educational, and housing support.

Finally, nonhuman friendships can also play a role in the lives of individuals with schizophrenia. Pets, especially dogs, offer unconditional love and companionship without the complexities of human interaction. Dogs don't care if their owners struggle with hallucinations or confusion—they provide comfort and companionship. Many families and hospitals have recognized the benefits of pets for people with schizophrenia, bringing joy and comfort to those who might otherwise feel alone.

CHAPTER 3: LIVING WITH SCHIZOPHRENIA

MANAGING SYMPTOMS IN EVERYDAY LIFE

Living with schizophrenia presents unique challenges that affect daily life. Managing symptoms consistently is crucial for maintaining stability and improving overall quality of life. Every day can bring new hurdles, from navigating delusions to staying focused on simple tasks. However, learning how to cope with symptoms effectively makes it possible to live a more balanced life. In this section, we will explore the common symptoms of schizophrenia, how they impact everyday activities, and some practical strategies to manage them. These tools can help create more structure and ease the difficulties that come with living with schizophrenia.

Schizophrenia is characterized by a range of symptoms, including delusions, hallucinations, disorganized thinking, and cognitive difficulties. These symptoms can vary from person to person but often make daily functioning difficult. For example, delusions might make someone believe something that isn't real, like feeling persecuted or thinking they have extraordinary powers. Hallucinations can involve hearing or seeing things that aren't present. Disorganized thinking may manifest as confusing speech or difficulty following a conversation. Cognitive issues like trouble with memory or decision-making can interfere with daily routines and responsibilities.

The symptoms of schizophrenia can significantly disrupt day-to-day life. Simple tasks, such as maintaining a routine or managing self-care, become challenging when dealing with hallucinations or paranoia. Social interactions may feel overwhelming, leading to withdrawal from friends and family. Work or school responsibilities can be hard to keep up with due to concentration issues or confusion. Decision-making may feel impossible when delusions or disorganized thoughts are strong. These symptoms create a cycle of frustration, making it difficult to maintain stability. Understanding how these challenges appear in everyday life makes it easier to develop strategies for managing them.

STRATEGIES FOR DEALING WITH STRESS AND TRIGGERS

Managing stress and identifying triggers are crucial for people with schizophrenia. Stress can intensify symptoms like delusions, hallucinations, or disorganized thinking. Even everyday situations can become overwhelming. That's why it's important to learn how to handle stress and pinpoint triggers before they escalate symptoms. In this section, I'll discuss practical strategies for managing stress and how to spot and reduce the impact of triggers. These techniques can help reduce the frequency and severity of symptom flare-ups, making day-to-day life more manageable.

Stress is closely linked to symptom flare-ups in schizophrenia. When stress levels rise, symptoms like paranoia, delusions, and cognitive difficulties tend to worsen. High-stress situations—at work, during social interactions, or sudden environmental changes—can cause a spike in symptoms. Even seemingly small stressors, like being in a noisy place, can sometimes serve as a trigger. Recognizing the connection between stress and symptoms is the first step toward preventing these flare-ups.

Everyone has personal triggers that worsen their symptoms. For some, it may be overstimulation or a lack of sleep; for others, it could be an emotionally charged situation. Identifying these triggers is key. A trigger journal can help pinpoint when symptoms tend to flare up and what might be causing them. This allows for better preparation and management in the future. By understanding personal triggers, individuals can take proactive steps to minimize stress and prevent symptoms from escalating.

Managing stress is essential for people with schizophrenia. Mindfulness, physical exercise, and relaxation routines can relieve and improve overall mental well-being. Practicing these techniques regularly can help reduce anxiety, calm the mind, and create a sense of stability, which is especially important when dealing with the challenges of schizophrenia.

Mindfulness is a powerful tool for managing stress. By staying present in the moment, individuals can avoid being overwhelmed by anxious thoughts. Simple mindfulness techniques like deep breathing, body scanning, and meditation are great ways to calm the mind. For example, mindful breathing involves focusing on each breath as it flows in and out of the body. This practice helps shift attention away from stress and toward the present moment. Another helpful technique is progressive muscle relaxation, where you consciously tense and then relax different muscle groups, releasing physical tension. These exercises are easy to incorporate into daily life and can be practiced anytime stress begins to build.

Regular physical activity is one of the most effective ways to reduce stress. Exercise releases endorphins, which improve mood and reduce anxiety. It also promotes better sleep, which can be especially beneficial for those dealing with schizophrenia. Simple exercises like walking, yoga, or light cardio can greatly improve mental health. Walking outside in nature for 15-30 minutes daily can provide a refreshing break and a sense of peace. Yoga is another excellent option, combining gentle stretching with deep breathing to promote relaxation. The key is to find enjoyable activities that fit comfortably into a daily routine.

Building a personal relaxation routine can help create a consistent space for unwinding. This routine might include calming activities like reading, listening to music, or engaging in hobbies that bring joy. Whether painting, writing, or watching a favorite movie, these activities distract from stressful thoughts and help refocus the mind on positive experiences. Setting aside time each day for relaxation is important, even in a busy schedule. This could be as simple as spending 10 minutes with a cup of tea in a quiet space or taking a warm bath before bed. Creating a daily calm routine can make a significant difference in managing stress and improving overall mental health.

Managing triggers in schizophrenia often requires a thoughtful approach to challenging negative thought patterns and delusional beliefs. Cognitive Behavioral Techniques (CBT) can be incredibly effective in helping individuals stay grounded, maintain perspective, and navigate stressful moments.

One of the key components of CBT is cognitive restructuring, a technique that helps individuals identify and challenge negative thought patterns. Often, these thoughts can distort reality, leading to stress, anxiety, or even delusional thinking. The first step is to recognize when negative thoughts arise. For example, if you think, "Everyone is against me," cognitive restructuring encourages you to pause and question that belief. Ask yourself: What evidence supports this thought? What evidence contradicts it? You can replace these distortions with healthier, reality-based thinking by actively challenging them. Instead of "Everyone is against me," you might reframe it as "I may feel anxious, but that doesn't mean others are actively working against me."

Reality testing is another useful technique, especially when managing delusional thoughts. It involves questioning beliefs that may not be grounded in reality and seeking confirmation from trusted sources. For instance, if you believe someone is spying on you, ask yourself: What concrete evidence do I have to support this belief? Can I verify it with someone I trust, like a close friend or therapist? Reality testing encourages you to differentiate between thoughts rooted in paranoia and what is happening. This practice can help reduce stress by encouraging a more logical and fact-based approach to managing delusions.

Coping statements are another powerful tool for managing stress and triggers. You can repeat These positive, affirming phrases to yourself during difficult times. Coping statements remind you of your strength and ability to handle stress. For example, you could say, "This is just a moment, and it will pass," or "I've managed stress before, and I can do it again." These statements help interrupt the cycle of negative thinking, offering reassurance and calming the mind. Incorporating these simple affirmations into your daily routine reinforces the belief that you can manage your mental health, even in the face of challenges.

These CBT strategies provide practical ways to manage the stress and triggers that can exacerbate schizophrenia symptoms. By recognizing negative thoughts, testing reality, and using coping statements, you can take control of your mental health, reducing the impact of stress on your daily life.

Creating a calm and supportive environment is essential for managing schizophrenia triggers. A peaceful living space helps reduce stress and fosters mental clarity. One key strategy is decluttering—keeping your space organized and free of excess items can create a sense of calm. Reducing noise by limiting distractions like loud TVs or disruptive sounds contributes to a supportive environment. It's helpful to designate a relaxation area within your home where you can meditate, read, or practice calming exercises whenever stress levels rise.

Setting boundaries is equally important for protecting your mental health. Clear, assertive boundaries with family, friends, and coworkers can help prevent stressful situations from escalating. Communicating your needs openly reduces the likelihood of feeling overwhelmed by others' demands or misunderstandings. This helps create a protective space where your mental health remains a priority. When set effectively, boundaries allow you to manage your relationships and maintain emotional stability.

Support systems play a major role in managing stress and triggers. Family and friends can provide emotional support when things get tough. They can also help you recognize triggers early on or offer healthy distractions. It is vital to communicate with loved ones about what stresses you out and how they can assist. When everyone is on the same page, you have a reliable support network to lean on during challenging times.

Professional support is just as important. Regular sessions with a therapist or psychiatrist allow you to develop personalized strategies for managing stress. Support groups provide a safe space to share experiences with others who understand. These professionals offer guidance and check-ins that help you stay on track, making stress management a more sustainable practice.

CHAPTER 4: THE TREATMENT OF SCHIZOPHRENIA

Schizophrenia, though often misunderstood, is treatable. Many people believe that once someone has been diagnosed with schizophrenia, there is little that can be done. This is not true. While it may not be curable in the traditional sense, effective treatments can help manage the symptoms and improve quality of life. Think of schizophrenia like diabetes. Both are chronic conditions that require ongoing management rather than a one-time cure. In the same way that someone with diabetes takes insulin to regulate their blood sugar, someone with schizophrenia often uses medication to help manage their symptoms.

Treatment is an ongoing process, often involving a combination of approaches. Medication is key, but therapy, community support, and lifestyle changes also play important roles. The goal is to help people regain stability and move forward in life despite the challenges of the illness.

It's important to understand that treatment takes time and often requires adjustments. What works for one person might not work for another. The key is finding the right combination that allows symptom control and provides a path to a better life. With the right support, people with schizophrenia can make significant strides in their journey toward well-being.

HOW TO FIND A GOOD DOCTOR

Finding a good doctor for treating schizophrenia can be a challenge, especially for family members and friends who are trying to help. Unfortunately, there aren't many doctors who specialize in or have a deep understanding of schizophrenia. This is disheartening because it's one of the most significant mental health conditions worldwide. However, even though the search may be tough, it's essential because schizophrenia requires proper medical treatment.

Schizophrenia is a biological illness, and medication plays a big role in managing its symptoms. So, at some point, a doctor needs to be involved. The doctor will not only prescribe medication but also help rule out other possible conditions, like brain tumors or infections that might be mimicking schizophrenia. That's why the initial diagnosis is so important—only a doctor can make sure it's schizophrenia.

One of the best ways to find a competent doctor is by asking other healthcare professionals for recommendations. Doctors and nurses know who is good in their field and are usually willing to share that information. Don't hesitate to ask for advice if you know someone who works in healthcare, even if it's a distant connection. Another helpful approach is to talk to other families who have been through similar situations. They can offer valuable insights into local resources and point you in the right direction.

On the other hand, referral lists from medical associations or local psychiatric groups may not always be useful. These lists often include doctors who are simply looking for more patients, regardless of their expertise in schizophrenia. It's better to rely on personal recommendations from people who know the field well.

When choosing a doctor, look for someone who combines skill with empathy and is open to working with the patient's family and a broader care team. Schizophrenia treatment often involves not just doctors but also psychologists, nurses, and social workers. A good doctor will be part of a team and willing to collaborate. It's also helpful to ask the doctor direct questions, such as their thoughts on the causes of schizophrenia and their experience with specific medications. These conversations can give you a sense of how up-to-date the doctor is with current treatments and whether they fit your needs.

HOSPITALIZATION

When someone with schizophrenia becomes acutely ill, hospitalization is often necessary. Hospitalization allows mental health professionals to observe the person in a controlled environment. In this setting, tests can be run to rule out other medical conditions, psychological assessments can be performed, and medications can be safely administered. Hospitalization also gives families a break after what is often a stressful and difficult time leading up to the acute episode.

Another reason for hospitalization is safety. Some individuals may try to harm themselves or others because of their illness. For example, someone might hear voices telling them to do something dangerous. In such cases, hospitalization provides the protection needed to prevent serious harm. Many hospitals use locked wards to ensure patient safety; sometimes, additional restraints are necessary. These measures are temporary, often lasting only a few hours until the medication starts to work. While some criticize using restraints, they remain essential in certain cases until better treatments are available.

There are other benefits to hospitalization beyond observation and safety. Psychiatric units often provide group therapy, occupational therapy, and recreational activities. These activities help patients see that they are not alone in their experiences. However, the most important factor in recovery is the proper use of medication to address acute symptoms.

ALTERNATIVES TO HOSPITALIZATION

While hospitalization is often necessary for those experiencing schizophrenia for the first time, alternatives exist for individuals who have already been diagnosed and are facing a relapse. These options sometimes help prevent hospitalization, especially when handled quickly and effectively.

One common alternative is receiving medication by injection at an emergency room or clinic. In many cases, a skilled physician can help reduce psychotic symptoms in a few hours, allowing the person to go home the same day. However, this option isn't always ideal for families exhausted by their loved one's recent behavior. In those situations, families may prefer a break and find it difficult to bring the person home immediately.

Mobile treatment teams offer another option. These teams visit the person at home, assess the situation, and often start treatment on the spot. This method can reduce the need for hospitalization, but it works best when there is follow-up care by skilled professionals coordinating ongoing treatment.

In some places, states and counties use short-term psychiatric beds in facilities other than hospitals. These institutions, sometimes called IMDs (Institutions for Mental Diseases) or crisis homes, provide a less expensive alternative to hospitalization. While these facilities might not be hospitals, they offer similar services and care.

Home treatment is also possible, where nurses or doctors visit patients at home. This method is used more frequently in countries like England, but there have also been successful cases in the United States. In one study, home visits and medication proved as effective as hospitalization. While home treatment can be intensive, involving regular visits for injections or monitoring, it may be preferred by some families.

Partial hospitalization is another effective alternative. In this approach, patients spend part of their day at the hospital but return home for the night. Day hospitals, where patients attend during the day, and night hospitals, where patients come in only to sleep, can be helpful for those needing structured care without full-time hospitalization. Unfortunately, these options are less common in the U.S., mainly due to restrictions on federal funding.

Each of these alternatives offers a way to manage schizophrenia symptoms while potentially avoiding a full hospital stay. However, they depend on the availability of resources and the specific needs of the person and their family.

THE REHABILITATION OF SCHIZOPHRENIA

The rehabilitation of schizophrenia focuses on helping individuals manage their lives despite the limitations of their condition. Rehabilitation is essential because treating schizophrenia with medication alone is rarely enough. Just as someone with a physical disability needs tools and training to adapt, people with schizophrenia need structured support to help them live independently and manage daily tasks.

The key to successful rehabilitation is providing opportunities for individuals with schizophrenia to regain as much functionality as possible. Although not everyone will fully recover, the better the support and opportunities, the better the person will likely manage their condition. This concept is similar to how we approach physical disabilities: we offer tools, adaptations, and emotional support to help people live fulfilling lives.

People with schizophrenia face several challenges, including managing finances, securing food and housing, finding employment, maintaining friendships, and accessing ongoing medical care. These areas of life require targeted rehabilitation efforts. Each person's needs will vary based on the severity of their symptoms, but addressing these fundamental challenges is critical to improving their quality of life.

Underlying all these efforts is one critical concept: hope. Hope is the foundation of rehabilitation. If someone believes they can improve their situation, they are more likely to succeed in rehabilitation. Without hope, even the best support systems are likely to fail. Studies show that when individuals feel optimistic about their future, they can better cope with their illness and achieve better outcomes.

THE RECOVERY MODEL

In recent years, the recovery model for treating schizophrenia has gained significant popularity. Many mental health professionals and organizations have embraced it, almost becoming a guiding principle. The model has its strengths and weaknesses, but the downsides are often overlooked.

One of the positive aspects of the recovery model is that it encourages people with schizophrenia to play a more active role in their treatment. The model emphasizes personal empowerment, setting goals, and fostering hope. It shifts the focus from passive treatment in institutional settings to self-direction and taking control of one's life. Through recovery, patients are encouraged to seek meaningful employment, develop social skills, and secure proper housing—important elements of rehabilitation. The model also highlights success stories, like that of Dr. Frederick Frese, a psychologist who made significant contributions to the field despite living with schizophrenia. Such examples provide hope to others.

However, there are problems with the recovery model as well. The model can be misleading, implying that everyone with schizophrenia can recover without clearly defining what recovery means. Often, those who champion the recovery model are individuals who have experienced milder forms of schizophrenia or whose symptoms have responded well to treatment. They may say, "If I recovered, so can you," which can be discouraging for those who struggle with more severe symptoms or who do not respond well to medications. For these individuals, the pressure to recover can make them feel that their inability to do so is somehow their fault, which is not helpful.

A more serious issue is that the recovery model tends to overlook individuals with severe symptoms, particularly those with anosognosia. These individuals are unaware of their illness due to the brain's impairment caused by schizophrenia. The recovery model's emphasis on self-direction does not apply to them. Asking a person with anosognosia to define their goals can result in responses like, "I want the CIA to stop following me" or "I need to get rid of the transmitter in my head." They may deny their need for treatment entirely, which makes self-directed recovery impossible.

For around half of people with schizophrenia, the recovery model does not offer a viable path. If any other medical condition—like breast cancer or diabetes—had a treatment model that ignored half of the affected population, there would be widespread outrage. However, in the case of schizophrenia, this issue has largely been ignored by advocates, leaving a significant portion of those affected without a clear path forward.

CHAPTER 5: SELF-TREATMENT: STRATEGIES FOR COPING

ROLE OF PRAYER AND READING THE BIBLE

Faith and religion play a big role in helping people cope with mental health challenges. For me, prayer and reading the Bible were like lifelines during some of the hardest times in my life. My faith gave me something to hold onto when everything felt out of control.

I wasn't alone in this—many people with schizophrenia find comfort and strength through their religious beliefs. Faith provides a sense of peace when the world feels overwhelming. In this chapter, I will explore how faith helped me cope with schizophrenia and how religious practices, like prayer and Bible reading, can offer hope to others facing similar struggles.

Faith is often more than just a belief system—it can be a source of strength and purpose, especially for people dealing with mental health issues like schizophrenia. In my experience, faith gave me something to lean on when everything else seemed uncertain. When the paranoia and fear took over, I turned to prayer. It was a simple act, but it helped ground me. Talking to God made me feel like someone was listening, even when I felt isolated.

Religious practices, like attending church or reading the Bible, gave me structure. They offered guidance when I couldn't find it anywhere else. It's not just about the rituals—it's about the hope that comes with believing in something bigger than yourself. Faith offers comfort and meaning when the mind is struggling to find peace.

For me, prayer has always been more than just words. It's a way of connecting with God, even when everything else feels out of control. During my most difficult moments, prayer became a refuge—a place where I could find peace and comfort, even for a little while. It wasn't about finding immediate answers. It was more about feeling like I wasn't alone in what I was going through. That connection to a higher power gave me hope when hope felt out of reach.

I remember during some of my worst psychotic episodes when paranoia and fear were overwhelming, I would turn to prayer. The act of praying helped calm my mind, even if the voices in my head were still loud. Talking to God helped me get through those episodes more strongly. I've heard similar stories from others with mental health struggles.

Prayer doesn't just provide spiritual comfort—it helps create a sense of control when life feels uncontrollable. It's a moment to pause, breathe, and focus on something beyond our struggles. It may not take the pain away, but it gives us the strength to keep moving forward. The connection to a higher power through prayer is powerful in ways that are hard to explain unless you've experienced it yourself.

Incorporating prayer into daily life can be a stabilizing force. It doesn't have to be complicated or long. Starting the day with a simple morning prayer helps me set the tone. It's like taking a moment to center myself before everything else starts. Gratitude prayers are also a great way to end the day. Even on the hardest days, I try to think of one or two things I'm thankful for and bring that into my prayers. Sometimes, just thinking about what I'm grateful for helps shift my mindset.

Another practice I've found helpful is meditative prayer. It's different from the traditional prayers I grew up with. Meditative prayer is more about quieting my mind and being present with God. It helps me manage my stress and reminds me to let go of things I can't control. I sit in a quiet space, close my eyes, and focus on breathing deeply. In those moments, I feel more at peace.

Prayer doesn't have to look the same for everyone. Some people pray aloud, others in silence. The important thing is to make it a consistent part of your routine. It's been a stabilizing force, something I can rely on when everything else feels shaky. Whether it's a short morning prayer, a quiet moment of gratitude, or meditative prayer, finding that connection each day has made a big difference in how I cope with my mental health.

READING THE BIBLE FOR SPIRITUAL RESILIENCE

The Bible has always comforted and guided me, especially during tough times. Turning to scripture helped me find some peace when my mind felt unraveling. The words within the Bible offered wisdom that seemed to calm my thoughts, reminding me that I wasn't alone in my struggles. For anyone going through mental health challenges, the Bible can be a place of refuge. It speaks of healing, strength, and resilience, which we all need when life feels overwhelming.

There are specific verses that have been particularly meaningful to me. Psalm 23 has always comforted me, especially the line, *"Even though I walk through the darkest valley, I will fear no evil, for you are with me."* That verse reminded me that God was with me no matter how deep my fear or paranoia went. Isaiah 41:10 was another verse I turned to often: *"Do not fear, for I am with you; do not be dismayed, for I am your God."* It reminded me that I didn't have to face them alone, even in my darkest moments. And then there's Philippians 4:13, *"I can do all things through Christ who strengthens me."* That simple verse became a mantra for me. Whenever I felt weak or overwhelmed, it reminded me that strength could come from my faith.

Reading the Bible doesn't just provide comfort—it builds mental resilience. Scripture reinforces positive thinking and gives us a way to counter negative thoughts, fear, or paranoia. There were many times when I was caught in a spiral of negative thinking. I would believe that everyone was against me or that my situation would never improve. But reading certain passages helped me pull myself out of that spiral. The words reminded me to trust in something greater, to hold on to hope even when it seemed impossible. The Bible became more than just a religious text; it became a tool for resilience.

Incorporating Bible study into my daily life has helped keep me grounded. It doesn't have to be complicated. Sometimes, I start my mornings by reading a verse and reflecting on it for a few minutes. Other times, I spend longer with scripture, diving deeper into its meaning. Group Bible study has also been helpful. Discussing the verses with others gives me different perspectives and creates a sense of community. Bible apps are another great way to stay connected to scripture throughout the day. They offer daily devotionals and reminders that keep me focused on my spiritual journey.

Applying the lessons of the Bible to everyday life has been key in managing stress and emotions. When I feel anxious, I think back to the verses that tell me to trust in God and not be afraid. When I feel lost, I remember the teachings about finding strength through faith. It's not just about reading the words—it's about living them. The Bible reminds me that no matter what happens, I have a source of resilience that can carry me through the challenges.

FAITH IN COMMUNITY

Being part of a church community has comforted and supported me during some of my toughest times. Attending church isn't just about worship—it's about connecting with others who share the same faith. When I walked through the doors of my church, I felt less alone. The people there didn't just offer prayers; they offered a sense of belonging. This emotional and social support became a lifeline for me.

Pastors and religious mentors play a special role in this community. My pastor helped guide me when I felt lost, offering wisdom and prayer that gave me strength. Fellow congregants also lifted me. Their prayers and encouragement made me feel part of something larger than myself. It's amazing how much healing can happen just by knowing others are praying for you and standing with you in faith.

Participating in group prayer and collective worship brought a sense of peace I couldn't always find alone. There's something powerful about being in a room full of people, all focused on the same hope and faith. It reminds me that we're all in this together, and no matter how isolated I might feel, I am never truly alone.

I encourage you to explore faith-based practices in your mental health journey. Whether through prayer, scripture, or fellowship, these practices can help you find strength and healing. You are not alone; faith can be a steady anchor during life's storms.

FINDING SOLACE AND STRENGTH IN SPIRITUALITY

Spirituality can be a powerful tool for coping with life's challenges, especially for those living with mental health conditions like schizophrenia. Unlike organized religion, spirituality is more about personal connection—whether to a higher power, nature, or an inner sense of peace. It doesn't follow strict rules or rituals; it offers flexibility and freedom to explore what feels right for each individual. For people dealing with schizophrenia, finding solace in spirituality can provide comfort, hope, and a sense of purpose during difficult times.

Spirituality is often described as a connection to something greater than ourselves. For some, that may mean connecting with a higher power or deity; for others, it may be about finding meaning in nature or developing a deep inner peace. In the context of mental health, spirituality can help individuals navigate the emotional storms that accompany conditions like schizophrenia. It's a way of grounding ourselves, seeking comfort, and finding clarity amid confusion.

The beauty of spirituality is that it's deeply personal. There's no single path or right way to experience it. Some people find spirituality in religious practices, while others connect with it through meditation, nature walks, or quiet reflection. What matters most is that it brings a sense of calm and strength to those who embrace it. For people dealing with schizophrenia, spirituality can serve as a guiding light during times of darkness, offering a sense of purpose when the world feels chaotic.

SPIRITUALITY VS. RELIGION

While spirituality and religion may seem similar, they are not the same. Religion is typically organized, with set beliefs, practices, and rituals that followers adhere to. Spirituality, on the other hand, is more open and flexible. It doesn't require a belief in a specific religion or a structured set of practices. Instead, spirituality is about personal growth and connection—whether with a higher power, nature or even one's inner self.

For people with schizophrenia, spirituality is an important tool for finding peace without the pressures of religious rules or expectations. It's a way to tap into something greater without conforming to a specific tradition. By focusing on spiritual growth and inner strength, people can find new ways to cope with the challenges of mental health.

MINDFULNESS AS A SPIRITUAL PRACTICE

Mindfulness is about being fully present in the moment aware of our thoughts, feelings, and surroundings without judgment. For people with schizophrenia, mindfulness helps anchor the mind during times of crisis. By focusing on the present, it becomes easier to separate reality from delusions and calm the anxiety that often comes with mental health struggles. Mindfulness helps reduce feeling overwhelmed and brings a sense of control, even when life feels chaotic.

In my own experience, practicing mindfulness has helped lessen the intensity of delusional thinking. It brings me back to the present, reminding me I'm safe and here. For those with schizophrenia, mindfulness can improve emotional regulation, making it easier to navigate through intense emotions and stress.

Meditation takes mindfulness a step further, creating a space to connect with our spiritual selves and find inner peace. There are many types of meditation, each offering its benefits. Breathwork meditation focuses on deep, controlled breathing, helping to calm the mind and body. Guided meditation, where a narrator leads the listener through a calming journey, can provide relaxation and a break from racing thoughts. Loving-kindness meditation encourages the development of compassion for ourselves and others, which can help combat feelings of isolation or anger.

Meditation offers more than just relaxation—it promotes mental clarity. By regularly meditating, I've found that my mind feels clearer and less cluttered by stress or anxiety. This clarity helps me make better decisions and feel more in control of my mental health. It's not a cure but a powerful tool for finding calm in the storm.

Building a daily mindfulness or meditation routine doesn't have to be complicated. Start small, maybe with five minutes of mindful breathing in the morning or before bed. Find a quiet space where you won't be disturbed, and focus on your breath or a specific sound. Gradually, you can extend the practice to longer sessions as you become more comfortable.

There are many resources to help you along the way. Meditation apps, like Headspace or Calm, offer guided meditations and daily reminders to practice. Mindfulness journals can also be helpful, allowing you to reflect on your experiences and track your progress. If you prefer community support, consider joining a meditation group, either in person or online, where you can connect with others who share similar goals.

Making mindfulness and meditation a regular part of your life can lead to greater emotional balance and a stronger connection to your spiritual self. It's a simple but powerful way to manage mental health and stay grounded.

CONNECTING WITH NATURE AND THE UNIVERSE

Spending time in nature has always had a calming effect on me. Something is refreshing about being outdoors, surrounded by trees, fresh air, and open skies. For people with schizophrenia, nature can offer a sense of peace that is hard to find elsewhere. It's a spiritual experience in itself. Being in nature helps me feel more connected to the world around me. It eases the feelings of isolation that often come with mental health struggles. Outside, I feel more grounded, and my mind feels clearer.

Beyond the peace of nature, I've also found strength in thinking about the universe. Feeling connected to a larger cosmic force gives me perspective. It reminds me that my challenges are just a small part of something bigger. This perspective helps me reframe my struggles. Instead of feeling overwhelmed by my problems, I see them as part of a larger journey. The universe has its rhythms, and being connected brings a sense of purpose and meaning that goes beyond daily struggles.

Incorporating nature into spiritual practice doesn't have to be complicated. Walking in the park, hiking through a forest, or simply sitting quietly outdoors can make a difference. These activities allow me to reflect and connect with the world around me. Another helpful practice is journaling about my feelings while in nature. Writing down my thoughts after spending time outside deepens the experience and helps me process emotions. These simple acts help me feel more connected and at peace.

Creating personal spiritual rituals has been a calming and grounding practice for me. Simple acts like lighting candles, setting up a peaceful space, or journaling can offer stability during hard times. These rituals create a moment of calm, helping me feel more centered and in control. When everything around me feels overwhelming, these small, intentional acts provide comfort. They give me a way to manage my emotions and offer a structure that I can return to whenever I need it.

Rituals don't have to be complicated. They can be as simple as sitting in a quiet room, lighting a candle, and reflecting on the day. For me, journaling is also a big part of this practice. Writing down my thoughts allows me to process my feelings and release some of the tension I hold onto. These rituals offer a grounding force that helps me stay connected to myself, even when everything feels out of balance.

Beyond personal rituals, I've also explored alternative healing practices like Reiki, sound therapy, and using crystals. Reiki, a form of energy healing, has helped me feel more balanced and at peace. The practice focuses on channeling energy to promote emotional and physical healing. Similarly, sound therapy, which involves listening to soothing sounds or vibrations, has calmed me during anxious moments.

I've also heard stories from others who have found comfort in these alternative methods. Some people use crystals to enhance their spiritual energy and help balance emotions. While these practices may not work for everyone, they can offer additional support for those seeking spiritual healing.

Spiritual mentors can be a valuable source of guidance and support during difficult times. Connecting with someone like a spiritual counselor or meditation teacher can provide insight when we feel lost. These mentors have experience in navigating life's challenges and offer wisdom to help us cope with mental health struggles.

Spiritual mentors don't just guide—they listen. They provide a safe space to explore emotions and fears without judgment. For people dealing with mental health conditions like schizophrenia, this support can be crucial. Knowing that someone understands your spiritual journey can bring comfort and relief.

Beyond individual mentors, spiritual communities can offer a sense of belonging. Whether online or in person, these groups allow us to share experiences and connect with others on a similar path. Online forums, meditation groups, and local meetups provide a space to explore spirituality together. These communities create an atmosphere of support, where people lift each other and offer encouragement during difficult times.

Being part of a spiritual community brings comfort and a sense of shared purpose. Connecting with others who understood my struggles helped me feel more grounded and supported.

Whether through personal rituals, community support, or alternative healing methods, exploring spirituality may lead to greater peace and resilience. I encourage you to find what works for you and allow spirituality to comfort you on your journey.

SELF-BELIEF AND MENTAL RESILIENCE

Self-belief and mental resilience are essential when navigating the challenges of mental health, particularly for individuals coping with schizophrenia. Believing in oneself means having confidence in your ability to face and grow from adversity. This belief plays a key role in building mental resilience, which is the ability to recover from setbacks and maintain emotional balance during difficult times. Without self-belief, it can be easy to feel defeated when confronted with the ups and downs of life.

In this section, I'll discuss the importance of self-belief in managing schizophrenia and the direct impact it has on mental resilience. We will explore what self-belief means, how it supports mental resilience, and practical ways to foster these qualities in your life.

Self-belief is the inner confidence that you have what it takes to face challenges and overcome them. For people with schizophrenia, it's about trusting that you can handle the unpredictable nature of your mental health. Self-belief isn't about ignoring the difficulties but accepting them while knowing you have the strength to move forward. It is the belief that no matter how hard things get, you can continue to make progress.

Mental resilience is the ability to bounce back from adversity and cope with stress effectively. It's what allows you to keep going when life feels overwhelming. For individuals dealing with mental health conditions, resilience is an important tool. It helps prevent setbacks from becoming permanent obstacles. The connection between self-belief and mental resilience is strong—when you believe in yourself, you're more likely to persevere through tough times and find ways to manage your mental health. Self-belief fuels resilience, giving you the power to recover and continue pushing forward, even when life throws its hardest challenges.

Believing in oneself can be a powerful force when it comes to mental health recovery, especially for those living with schizophrenia. It's not always easy, but self-belief can be the turning point that makes recovery possible. When we believe that we can manage our condition, it helps us stay committed to treatment, whether medication, therapy, or other forms of care. Self-belief gives us hope and encourages us to keep moving forward, even on the hardest days. It allows us to see that recovery is possible and that we can achieve personal goals despite obstacles.

For instance, maintaining faith in my ability helped me stick with my treatment plan, even when it felt overwhelming. That belief helped me push through difficult moments and kept me focused on the small victories along the way. I could have easily given up without that belief, but knowing that I had the strength within me made all the difference.

On the other hand, negative self-perception can severely hinder progress in mental health recovery. When we doubt ourselves can create a cycle of hopelessness and helplessness. Self-doubt often leads to negative self-talk, where we convince ourselves that we're incapable of getting better or that nothing will ever improve. This mindset can make it harder to stay motivated and committed to recovery.

I've seen firsthand how lacking self-belief can keep someone stuck in their struggles. I read someone's story who was dealing with similar challenges but constantly told himself that he wasn't strong enough to overcome his symptoms. His negative thoughts became a barrier to his progress. Because he didn't believe in his ability to improve, he often skipped treatments and avoided reaching out for help. This only deepened his feelings of despair and delayed his recovery. Without self-belief, it's easy to lose sight of the possibility of change.

One of the most significant examples of self-belief playing a crucial role in recovery comes from a woman I met during a support group meeting. She had been diagnosed with schizophrenia a few years earlier and was initially overwhelmed by her condition. For a long time, she struggled with negative self-talk, telling herself she wasn't capable of living a normal life. It wasn't until she started working with a therapist who encouraged her to focus on building self-belief that things began to change.

Through small steps, she started to believe in her ability to manage her mental health. She began adhering to her treatment plan, setting personal goals, and celebrating each accomplishment, no matter how small. Her self-belief grew stronger, and with it, her mental resilience. Over time, she was able to regain control over her life, proving that self-belief can be a powerful tool in overcoming mental health challenges.

BUILDING SELF-BELIEF: PRACTICAL STEPS

SET SMALL, ACHIEVABLE GOALS

One of the most effective ways to build self-belief is by setting small, realistic goals. When we accomplish even the smallest task, it reinforces our confidence and helps us believe that bigger successes are possible. These small victories create momentum, making it easier to continue setting and reaching goals. It's about proving to yourself, little by little, that you can achieve what you set out to do.

For example, you might start by committing to a simple daily routine, such as getting out of bed at a set time each morning or preparing a healthy meal. You could also aim to participate in a social activity, even if it's just for a short time. Another achievable goal could be attending therapy sessions regularly. Each of these goals, though small, helps strengthen your self-belief. As you accomplish them, you build the foundation for tackling larger challenges.

POSITIVE AFFIRMATIONS AND VISUALIZATION

Positive affirmations and visualization techniques are powerful tools for strengthening self-belief over time. Affirmations are positive statements you say to yourself, designed to counter negative thoughts and build confidence. When you repeat affirmations regularly, they begin to reshape how you see yourself and your abilities.

Visualizing yourself overcoming challenges or reaching a goal reinforces self-belief by creating a mental image of success.

To get started, create personal affirmations that resonate with you, such as "I am capable of managing my mental health" or "I have the strength to handle life's challenges." Say these affirmations to yourself daily, ideally in front of a mirror, to make them more impactful. Visualization can be equally effective—spend a few minutes each day picturing yourself completing a task or overcoming a challenge. Practicing these techniques regularly makes you feel more confident handling difficult situations.

CHALLENGING NEGATIVE THOUGHTS

Negative thoughts are often the biggest obstacles to self-belief. Recognizing and challenging these thoughts is crucial for maintaining confidence in yourself. When you notice a negative thought creeping in, such as "I can't do this" or "I'm not good enough," take a moment to question its validity. Ask yourself if there's evidence to support that thought or if it's simply an assumption.

Cognitive restructuring is one strategy that can help with this. It involves identifying and replacing irrational thoughts with more balanced, realistic ones. For instance, if you think, "I'll never succeed," you could counter that with, "I've faced challenges before and made progress. I can do it again." Mindfulness can also help by encouraging you to stay present and focus on what's real rather than getting lost in negative thinking. By consistently challenging your negative thoughts, you weaken their power and strengthen your self-belief.

CULTIVATING MENTAL RESILIENCE IN DAILY LIFE

EMBRACING SETBACKS AS LEARNING OPPORTUNITIES

Setbacks are a part of life. No matter how prepared or determined we are, things don't always go according to plan. But instead of seeing setbacks as failures, mentally resilient people view them as opportunities to learn and grow. When we encounter obstacles, it's an invitation to reflect on what went wrong and figure out what can be done differently next time. Rather than dwelling on disappointment, we can reframe the situation to ask, "What can I learn from this?"

It's not always easy to adopt this mindset, especially when dealing with mental health challenges like schizophrenia. However, every setback can teach us something valuable about ourselves and our approach to life. Whether learning better coping strategies, understanding our triggers, or simply practicing patience with ourselves, setbacks become less daunting when we see them as stepping stones toward personal growth.

DEVELOPING A ROUTINE FOR MENTAL RESILIENCE

Establishing a routine is another key to building mental resilience. Routine creates a sense of stability and control, which is especially important when managing schizophrenia. A consistent daily structure allows us to anchor our minds and feel more grounded, even when life feels chaotic. Simple routines like setting regular times for meals, sleep, self-care, therapy, and exercise can help bring a sense of balance to our days.

To start, try scheduling small, manageable tasks that promote well-being. For example, set aside time in the morning for meditation or reflection, followed by a brief exercise session or stretching. Plan regular self-care moments, whether reading, taking a walk, or practicing mindfulness. Establishing a routine reinforces our resilience, creating a safe space where we feel more in control.

FOSTERING A GROWTH MINDSET

A growth mindset is the belief that our abilities and intelligence are not fixed but can be developed over time with effort and learning. Embracing this mindset is a powerful way to foster mental resilience. When we approach life with a growth mindset, setbacks are no longer seen as permanent roadblocks. Instead, they are viewed as opportunities to improve, adapt, and evolve.

A growth mindset means believing we can develop new skills, strategies, and strengths despite mental health challenges. It's a reminder that we are always learning and growing and that every experience—good or bad—contributes to our overall resilience. By adopting this mindset, we empower ourselves to keep pushing forward, knowing that setbacks are not failures but opportunities for improvement.

TECHNIQUES FOR MAINTAINING MENTAL HEALTH

Maintaining mental health for individuals living with schizophrenia is an ongoing process. Consistent effort and attention are required to manage symptoms and improve overall quality of life. One of the key aspects of managing schizophrenia is maintaining a routine that offers stability and support. This section will provide practical techniques to help maintain mental well-being daily. We'll explore the importance of having a structured routine and building healthy habits that promote stability, reduce anxiety, and foster a sense of control over daily life.

Establishing a consistent routine is crucial for those living with schizophrenia. Routines provide a sense of predictability that can be comforting, especially for those who may experience disorganized thinking or paranoia. Knowing what to expect each day helps reduce anxiety and allows individuals to focus on their tasks without being overwhelmed by uncertainty. A structured routine can improve concentration and make it easier to accomplish daily tasks, building confidence and a sense of achievement.

For someone with schizophrenia, even small changes in routine can cause stress or confusion. That's why it's important to create a manageable and flexible routine to accommodate any unexpected changes. Start by planning your day with fixed activities, such as waking up simultaneously, eating regular meals, and engaging in therapeutic activities or hobbies. The goal is to create a rhythm that keeps you grounded and gives you something to rely on when the world feels chaotic.

Incorporating healthy habits into your routine is just as important as maintaining it. Healthy habits provide a foundation for mental and physical well-being. Simple things, like establishing a regular sleep schedule and ensuring you get enough rest each night, are essential for mental health. Regular sleep can help regulate mood and reduce feelings of irritability or fatigue, which are common among individuals with schizophrenia.

Fixed meal times and balanced nutrition are equally important. Eating well provides the energy needed to function throughout the day and supports overall mental clarity. Self-care practices, such as maintaining good hygiene, exercising, and practicing relaxation techniques, are also essential. These habits don't have to be complicated. Something as simple as taking a walk, doing light stretches, or engaging in meditation can help create a sense of calm and improve emotional regulation.

By establishing a routine and incorporating healthy habits, individuals with schizophrenia can create a stable and supportive environment that nurtures both mental and physical health. It's a small but powerful step toward maintaining overall well-being.

COGNITIVE BEHAVIORAL TECHNIQUES

Cognitive Behavioral Therapy (CBT) is a valuable tool for managing symptoms of schizophrenia. It focuses on identifying and challenging distorted thought patterns, helping individuals replace them with healthier and more balanced ways of thinking. For those living with schizophrenia, this can be a game-changer. By understanding how certain thoughts are linked to delusions or paranoia, individuals can develop the skills needed to recognize triggers and manage them more effectively.

CBT empowers people to confront their negative or irrational thoughts head-on. For example, if someone experiences delusional thinking, such as believing they are being watched, CBT helps them question the evidence for that belief and assess it more rationally. Challenging and reframing thoughts builds mental resilience and offers greater control over symptoms.

One way to put CBT into practice is by engaging in simple exercises that can be done independently. Thought journaling is a helpful technique where individuals write down their thoughts and examine them for distortions or exaggerations. Cognitive restructuring involves identifying and replacing these distortions with more realistic, balanced thoughts. Another helpful exercise is relaxation techniques, such as deep breathing or progressive muscle relaxation, which can calm the mind and reduce anxiety when intrusive thoughts appear.

The goal of these exercises is to reframe negative thinking and develop healthier patterns of response. By practicing CBT regularly, individuals can gradually strengthen their ability to manage intrusive thoughts and cope with stress more effectively.

PHYSICAL HEALTH AND ITS CONNECTION TO MENTAL HEALTH

Physical activity plays a significant role in improving mental health, especially for individuals with schizophrenia. Regular exercise has been shown to reduce anxiety, enhance mood, and decrease the severity of schizophrenia symptoms. When you exercise, your body releases endorphins—natural chemicals that help elevate your mood and create a sense of well-being. Exercise can also improve your sleep patterns, essential for mental stability, and provide a healthy outlet for stress. Whether it's a simple walk, yoga, or light strength training, any form of movement can help calm your mind and boost your mental health.

Also, what you eat has a direct impact on your mental health. A balanced diet rich in nutrients supports brain function and emotional well-being. Staying hydrated and avoiding stimulants like caffeine, sugar, and alcohol is crucial for managing symptoms. Nutrient-dense foods, such as those rich in omega-3 fatty acids, leafy greens, and whole grains, help nourish the brain. Incorporating these brain-boosting foods into your meals can enhance mental clarity and promote emotional balance. Small changes, such as choosing whole grains over processed foods or drinking more water, can make a big difference.

BUILDING AND STRENGTHENING SUPPORT NETWORKS

A strong support system is essential for maintaining mental health, especially when living with schizophrenia. Family, friends, and mental health professionals provide the encouragement and stability needed during difficult times. Regular check-ins with loved ones, therapy appointments, and group meetings create a sense of security. A consistent support network can also help you navigate challenges, offering emotional comfort and practical assistance when needed.

Peer support groups offer a unique benefit to those living with schizophrenia by providing a safe space to connect with others who understand your challenges. Sharing experiences with peers who face similar struggles can empower and reassure you that you're not alone. You can find local or online support groups through mental health organizations, and regular participation can build a sense of community. These connections can provide a powerful source of strength as you work toward mental wellness.

CHAPTER 6: SPREADING AWARENESS

COMMON MISCONCEPTIONS ABOUT SCHIZOPHRENIA

Schizophrenia is one of the most misunderstood mental health conditions, and this misinformation can have harmful effects on those living with it. Common misconceptions often lead to stigma, discrimination, and a lack of empathy toward individuals who struggle with this illness. These misunderstandings can make it harder for people with schizophrenia to access the support and care they need, and they may face social isolation or fear of judgment.

In this section, we'll look at some of the most prevalent myths about schizophrenia and explain the reality behind them. By addressing these misconceptions, we hope to provide a clearer understanding of what it's really like to live with schizophrenia. Educating others about the truth of this condition is essential in reducing stigma and promoting acceptance.

One of the biggest challenges people with schizophrenia face is the overwhelming amount of misinformation surrounding the condition. These misconceptions fuel stigma and create unnecessary barriers to understanding and empathy. People often make assumptions about schizophrenia based on what they see in movies or hear from others, but these portrayals are usually far from the truth. Misunderstanding leads to fear, which in turn leads to isolation and discrimination.

For someone living with schizophrenia, this lack of understanding can be just as difficult to cope with as the symptoms themselves. I aim to address some of these common myths and provide clear, accurate information about what schizophrenia is—and what it is not. Through this, I hope to help others see that schizophrenia does not define a person. It's one part of their life, but they don't have to be limited. Educating others is key to changing the conversation around mental health and building a more supportive community.

One of the most harmful misconceptions about schizophrenia is the idea that people with the condition are violent or dangerous. This stereotype is often fueled by how movies, TV shows, and media portray individuals with mental illness, especially when they are linked to crimes or erratic behavior. Headlines tend to sensationalize these incidents, creating a lasting impression that schizophrenia and violence go hand in hand. However, these depictions are inaccurate and only add to the stigma.

The reality is that most people with schizophrenia are nonviolent. Studies show that individuals with schizophrenia are much more likely to be victims of violence than perpetrators. Schizophrenia, like many mental health conditions, can lead to confusion or fear, but this does not make someone inherently dangerous. With proper treatment and a strong support network, the vast majority of people with schizophrenia manage their symptoms well and pose no threat to others. Violent behavior is not common, especially when individuals receive the care they need.

To combat this misconception, it's important to share the true stories of people living with schizophrenia who lead peaceful, productive lives. These stories can help shift the narrative away from fear and toward understanding. By educating others and challenging the harmful stereotypes, we can create a more supportive and informed community for those affected by schizophrenia.

A common misconception about schizophrenia is that it renders a person incapable of living a functional life. Many believe that individuals with schizophrenia cannot hold jobs, maintain relationships, or participate in society due to their condition. This stereotype is harmful and completely overlooks the reality that people with schizophrenia, with the right treatment and support, can lead fulfilling and productive lives.

The truth is that many individuals with schizophrenia successfully work in a variety of professions, manage their responsibilities, and contribute positively to their communities. From artists and writers to educators and healthcare professionals, people with schizophrenia are achieving their goals and overcoming the challenges of their condition. Their success stories show that schizophrenia does not define a person's abilities or determine their potential.

Personal stories are a powerful way to educate others and combat this stereotype. When individuals share their experiences of living with schizophrenia and thriving despite the challenges, they humanize the condition and help shift perspectives. These real-life examples are key to breaking down the myth that schizophrenia limits intelligence or prevents someone from functioning in society.

A persistent misconception about schizophrenia is that it's caused by poor parenting or personal weakness. This belief blames families and individuals for something rooted in complex biological, genetic, and environmental factors. Schizophrenia is a mental health disorder with a well-documented scientific basis, not something triggered by how someone was raised or because they lack the willpower to manage their thoughts and emotions.

Perpetuating the idea that parenting or personal strength is responsible for schizophrenia causes unnecessary guilt and shame for both individuals and their families. It shifts focus away from the underlying causes and can prevent people from seeking the help they need. Families might wrongly believe they've failed, while individuals may feel inadequate or weak, adding to the emotional burden of living with the condition.

Educating others with scientifically accurate information is essential to correct this false narrative. Understanding that schizophrenia arises from a combination of genetics, brain chemistry, and external factors encourages a more empathetic perspective. This, in turn, helps dispel harmful myths and promotes better support for individuals and their families.

Educating the public about schizophrenia is one of the most effective ways to reduce stigma. When people understand the true nature of the condition, they are less likely to judge or discriminate against those who live with it. Knowledge creates a bridge to empathy and understanding.

Dispelling myths and spreading accurate information fosters a more supportive environment where individuals with schizophrenia can thrive. Challenging stereotypes can make society more inclusive, helping those affected feels less isolated and more accepted.

Misconceptions about schizophrenia have far-reaching effects on those who live with the condition. Addressing these misunderstandings is key to promoting a more informed, compassionate view. Whether it's debunking myths about causes, challenging ideas about violence, or highlighting the capabilities of those with schizophrenia, educating others is a powerful tool for change. By sharing accurate information and breaking down stereotypes, we can help create a world where individuals with schizophrenia are seen and supported for who they truly are.

IMPORTANCE OF MENTAL HEALTH AWARENESS

Mental health awareness is becoming more important in society today. By educating people about mental health, especially conditions like schizophrenia, we can break down the stigma that surrounds them. Awareness helps people feel more comfortable seeking support and opens the door to understanding these conditions. Talking openly about mental health encourages compassion and acceptance, creating an environment where those affected can thrive. This section will explore how mental health awareness reduces stigma, improves support systems, and benefits individuals and communities.

The stigma around mental health is rooted in fear, ignorance, and a lack of education. People often misunderstand mental illnesses like schizophrenia, assuming they are dangerous or untreatable. This stigma leads to isolation and discrimination for individuals living with these conditions, making it harder for them to reach out for help or share their struggles. It creates an environment where mental illness is hidden away, further reinforcing negative stereotypes and misconceptions.

Increasing awareness can change this. When more people understand mental health, they become more empathetic and supportive. Mental health campaigns and public figures have already made strides in breaking the stigma. Celebrities and advocates sharing their own experiences help to humanize mental illness, showing the world that it is not something to be feared or judged. This increased visibility helps normalize discussions about mental health, which in turn encourages more people to seek help when they need it.

Raising mental health awareness creates a ripple effect throughout society. When stigma is reduced, people with mental illnesses feel more comfortable discussing their experiences, leading to stronger support systems within families and workplaces. Awareness also fosters more inclusive communities, where individuals with mental health challenges are treated with respect and given opportunities to lead fulfilling lives.

Mental health awareness plays a key role in early detection of conditions like schizophrenia. When people are educated about common warning signs, they are more likely to recognize when something is wrong. Symptoms such as social withdrawal, changes in mood, and unusual thoughts can often go unnoticed. However, when these signs are understood, it can lead to faster diagnosis and treatment, helping individuals manage their condition before it escalates.

Awareness also promotes preventative care. It encourages people to take regular mental health check-ups seriously and engage in self-care practices that can prevent a crisis. Early intervention is crucial because it can stop symptoms from worsening. By being aware of the signs, people can seek help early, giving them a better chance at managing their mental health effectively.

Mental health awareness campaigns reduce the delay between the onset of symptoms and seeking treatment. In the past, people might have waited too long out of fear or uncertainty, worsening their condition. However, with better awareness, individuals are more likely to seek treatment sooner, improving their long-term outcomes.

Mental health awareness empowers people to take charge of their well-being. It encourages individuals to recognize when they need help and to seek support without shame. By promoting self-awareness and self-advocacy, people can reflect on their mental health, build resilience, and become advocates for themselves.

Awareness also helps remove barriers to treatment. Many people avoid seeking help because they fear judgment, don't know where to go, or feel confused about the process. Public awareness campaigns make mental health resources more accessible, reducing confusion and increasing the visibility of treatment options.

Open conversations about mental health are crucial. Awareness efforts promote these discussions, helping to normalize mental health struggles and reduce feelings of isolation. When people feel comfortable talking about their experiences, it creates a supportive community where no one feels alone.

Community-based awareness programs play a crucial role in spreading mental health awareness. Local organizations and communities often host events, workshops, and campaigns that educate the public about mental health issues. These initiatives create safe spaces for open discussions and provide resources that might otherwise be inaccessible. For example, some communities have organized mental health fairs or support groups that raise awareness and connect individuals with necessary services.

In the corporate world, mental health initiatives are equally important. Workplaces can offer mental health training, provide resources, and foster a supportive culture prioritizing employee well-being. Companies implementing mental health programs often see happier, healthier, and more productive employees. By recognizing the importance of mental well-being, businesses can reduce workplace stress and create a more inclusive environment where employees feel valued and supported.

Schools and universities also play a key role in promoting mental health awareness. Educational institutions can integrate mental health education into their curricula and offer support services to students. Programs that teach young people about mental health from an early age help break the cycle of stigma and empower students to seek help when needed. Many schools now offer counseling services and mental health workshops, providing students with the tools to manage their mental well-being throughout their lives.

Across the globe, there is a growing movement toward raising mental health awareness. Organizations like the World Health Organization (WHO) and Mental Health America are leading efforts to bring mental health issues to the forefront. Global awareness days, such as World Mental Health Day, have significantly contributed to shedding light on mental health concerns and encouraging conversations about them. These efforts have sparked international dialogue and have pushed for better mental health services worldwide.

The future of mental health awareness relies on maintaining this momentum. Continued efforts are essential, and individuals can play a role by sharing their stories, advocating for improved mental health services, and supporting awareness campaigns. Through collective action, we can create a future where mental health is treated equally to physical health, leading to better support for those who need it most.

Increased awareness helps break down barriers and fosters a more compassionate society. Together, we can build a world where those living with mental health conditions are supported and valued, making lasting improvements in the lives of millions.

PERSONAL EFFORTS TO SPREAD AWARENESS

Advocating for mental health awareness, particularly regarding schizophrenia, is a powerful way to make a difference. By sharing personal experiences and engaging in conversations, individuals can help reduce stigma, educate others, and create a more supportive environment for those living with schizophrenia. Advocacy doesn't have to be on a large scale—it can start with small, everyday efforts that contribute to broader change. This section will explore how individuals can become advocates and spread awareness through personal efforts.

One of the most impactful ways to spread awareness about schizophrenia is by sharing personal stories. Real-life experiences resonate with people in a way that statistics and medical explanations often can't. When individuals speak openly about their journey with schizophrenia, they make mental health issues more relatable, humanizing the condition and breaking down misconceptions. Personal stories help people see the reality behind the illness, dispelling myths that often fuel stigma.

Sharing your story can make a significant difference for you and others going through similar challenges. It lets them know they are not alone in their struggles, offering hope and a sense of community. Additionally, your story has the power to change minds, helping the broader public understand schizophrenia in a more nuanced way. When people hear real experiences, it challenges stereotypes and misconceptions, leading to greater empathy and acceptance.

There are many practical ways to share your story. You could write a blog post about your journey, participate in podcasts, or speak at mental health events. Social media is another powerful tool for advocacy. You can share your thoughts, challenges, and triumphs on Instagram, Facebook, or Twitter platforms. Videos and live discussions can also be a great way to reach a wider audience. Through these efforts, you can start conversations that spread awareness and foster understanding, meaningfully impacting how schizophrenia is perceived.

Grassroots advocacy can be one of the most effective ways to raise awareness about schizophrenia within local communities. When people take the initiative to start conversations and share knowledge on a smaller, more personal scale, it often creates ripples of understanding and empathy. By addressing mental health in everyday interactions, individuals help demystify schizophrenia, making it easier for others to understand the challenges faced by those living with the condition. Community-level advocacy is crucial for reducing stigma and building support networks.

Organizing mental health awareness events is another powerful way to promote understanding. Simple events like awareness walks, educational workshops, or panel discussions can bring people together to learn and share. Collaborating with local organizations, schools, or community centers can amplify these efforts, making the events more accessible and impactful. Whether hosting a small gathering or a larger public seminar, these events provide opportunities for education, conversation, and the exchange of personal stories, which can profoundly change perceptions.

In addition to organized events, one-on-one conversations can make a big difference in spreading awareness. Speaking with family, friends, and colleagues about schizophrenia helps them better understand the condition and reduces any misconceptions they may have. These informal discussions are vital in creating supportive environments, allowing individuals to feel heard and understood. By sharing accurate information and fostering empathy in your immediate circles, you can play a role in shaping a more compassionate community for those affected by schizophrenia.

Social media has become a powerful tool for spreading mental health awareness and educating the public about conditions like schizophrenia. Platforms such as Instagram, Twitter, Facebook, and TikTok allow advocates to connect with a wide audience, share their stories, and engage with mental health communities across the globe. By using these platforms, individuals can amplify their advocacy efforts, helping to reach people who might not otherwise be exposed to accurate information about mental health.

Effective online advocacy starts with being intentional in your approach. Use hashtags like #MentalHealthAwareness or #EndTheStigma to join broader conversations and reach more people. Share credible resources, mental health facts, and personal insights that help demystify schizophrenia. Consistency is key—regularly posting relevant content, engaging with your audience, and collaborating with other advocates will help you build momentum and make a lasting impact.

Social media is also an excellent platform for storytelling. Sharing personal experiences with schizophrenia, hosting live discussions, or creating Q&A sessions can be incredibly impactful. These interactions give people a chance to ask questions, learn, and better understand the realities of living with schizophrenia. Through storytelling and conversation, social media can be a space for education, empathy, and advocacy.

Partnering with local and national mental health organizations can amplify your advocacy efforts. Working with established groups provides a platform to reach more people and contribute to broader initiatives. By volunteering at events, participating in mental health campaigns, or helping with fundraising efforts, individuals can support vital programs and research for schizophrenia. These partnerships help spread awareness and provide resources to those in need.

Becoming an advocate through larger platforms is another impactful way to contribute. You can engage with organizations like NAMI (National Alliance on Mental Illness) or Mental Health America by becoming a speaker, writing for their platforms, or sharing their resources with your community. These larger groups offer opportunities to connect with a broader audience and help break the stigma surrounding schizophrenia on a bigger scale.

Additionally, consider becoming a mentor or peer supporter within these organizations. Offering guidance to those newly diagnosed or struggling with their mental health can be incredibly rewarding. Through mentorship and peer support, you advocate for mental health and provide a lifeline to someone who may feel isolated or overwhelmed. This type of advocacy directly and positively impacts people's lives, showing them they are not alone in their journey.

Educating others about schizophrenia is essential to breaking down misconceptions and reducing stigma. Through open dialogue, we can foster empathy and understanding. By leading with compassion and sharing accurate information, we can help those around us see schizophrenia for what it is—a medical condition that deserves support and care, not judgment or fear.

Personal advocacy plays a significant role in shifting societal perspectives on mental health. By challenging outdated views and promoting a more informed understanding of schizophrenia, we create a culture where people feel safe to seek help and live without stigma. Our efforts, though personal, contribute to a broader societal change.

CHAPTER 7: LOOKING TO THE FUTURE

PERSONAL GOALS AND ASPIRATIONS

As I look toward the future, my goals are rooted in both personal growth and continuing to help others. After my release, I worked hard to live normally, though it wasn't easy. Socializing again was a challenge; at first, I struggled to reconnect with people. But one day, I ran into an old friend at the gym, and from there, I began to open up more. It was a gradual process, but eventually, I found my way back into social circles, meeting new people and strengthening old bonds.

One of my biggest goals is to continue advancing my nursing career. I've been working as a nurse for two years, gaining valuable experience, and now I aim to become a registered nurse. It will take hard work, but I'm determined to reach that goal. Nursing is more than just a job to me—it's a way to give back and help others through their struggles, just as I've worked through mine.

Outside of nursing, I remain passionate about music, which has always been my outlet. Writing this book has also been a major focus, and I hope that by sharing my story, I can inspire others facing similar challenges. I want people to know that recovery is possible, and even when things seem bleak, there's a path forward.

In the future, I also dream of buying my own house and settling into a place I can call home. Building a stable, fulfilling life is something I've worked toward for years, and I'm finally seeing that vision come to life. Socially, I've come a long way too. There was a time when I couldn't imagine talking to girls or going out, but now I enjoy social settings again—whether at a bar or club or just hanging out with old and new friends. These connections have helped me heal and move forward.

Ultimately, my future is about growth, both personally and professionally. But it's also about helping others, whether through my work as a nurse, my music, or by sharing my story. I hope others can see my journey and find hope in their lives, knowing they aren't alone in their struggles.

Living with schizophrenia has taught me profound lessons—lessons that I believe can offer hope and guidance to anyone facing similar struggles. Reflecting on these experiences has given me the insight to understand that, no matter how tough life gets, there are always ways to overcome challenges. It may not be easy, but it's possible to find strength and stability even amid mental health difficulties. Through resilience, adaptability, and patience, I have learned that recovery is a journey that continues each day. I want to share these lessons with others, hoping they provide inspiration and hope for the road ahead.

1. THE IMPORTANCE OF RESILIENCE AND ADAPTABILITY

One of the most valuable lessons schizophrenia has taught me is the importance of resilience. There have been countless times when I've faced setbacks—whether from symptoms spiraling out of control, challenges with treatment, or even moments of hopelessness. Resilience means bouncing back from those setbacks and refusing to give up. I've had to learn to pick myself up after every episode, every difficult day, and keep moving forward. It wasn't something that came naturally—it took time and practice. But through each setback, I became stronger and better equipped to handle whatever came next.

Alongside resilience, adaptability has been key. Living with schizophrenia means navigating unpredictable symptoms and adjusting to new treatments as they come along. It's about learning to embrace change, even when it's uncomfortable. For me, adapting to change meant finding new ways to cope, staying open to treatments I wasn't initially comfortable with, and being flexible when life threw curveballs my way. When symptoms flared up, I had to learn to stay calm, grounded, and focus on what I could control. It's an ongoing process of learning to adjust to whatever life brings, and that adaptability has helped me move through tough times with more grace.

Resilience is not something you achieve once and then move on from. It's an ongoing journey that requires patience and consistent effort. Some days are easier than others, and that's okay. What's important is that each day, I remind myself that I have the strength to keep going. I want to pass on this journey of resilience and adaptability— because if I can make it through, so can others.

2. THE POWER OF SELF-ACCEPTANCE AND COMPASSION

Learning to embrace self-acceptance has been a significant part of my journey. It wasn't easy at first, but I realized that accepting my condition, my limitations, and my progress was key to finding peace within myself. Self-acceptance doesn't mean giving up or settling; it's about understanding that where you are today is okay. Accepting that I have schizophrenia doesn't mean I let it define me—it means I acknowledge it as part of my life while continuing to grow and improve. This mindset has helped reduce the self-criticism and feelings of inadequacy that often arise when I struggle with my symptoms.

Practicing self-compassion has also played a critical role in my mental health journey. In moments of difficulty, I've learned to be kinder to myself. I used to be incredibly hard on myself when things didn't go as planned, but I've understood that being harsh only makes it worse. Self-compassion means speaking to myself the way I would to a friend—gently and with understanding. I remind myself that it's okay to have bad days and that I don't have to be perfect. This kindness allows me to recover more quickly and prevents guilt and shame from overwhelming me. I use positive self-talk, setting realistic expectations, and permitting myself to rest when needed.

Self-acceptance isn't something you achieve overnight; it's a lifelong practice that continues to evolve. As I grow and learn more about myself, my understanding of self-acceptance deepens. There will always be ups and downs, but approaching them with acceptance and compassion helps me stay grounded. Accepting who I am—and being kind to myself in the process—has brought me greater emotional stability and peace.

3. THE VALUE OF SUPPORT NETWORKS AND CONNECTIONS

Leaning on others has been essential in my journey with schizophrenia. Meaningful connections with my family, friends, mentors, and mental health professionals have helped me stay grounded when things get tough. Their encouragement and understanding provide a sense of belonging, reminding me I'm not facing these challenges alone. Support networks offer comfort and the emotional stability needed to keep moving forward, even during my hardest moments.

Open communication has been key in maintaining these connections. Talking openly with those around me about what I'm going through makes a difference. It allows for honest conversations about my struggles and progress, helping them understand how best to support me. Building trust takes time, but it's strengthened by vulnerability and openness. It's about letting others in, even when it's hard, and allowing them to be part of the healing process.

Giving back to those who have supported me has also been important. I've learned that relationships are reciprocal—not just about receiving help but also about offering support in return. Being there for others when needed, sharing my experiences and lessons, and regularly expressing gratitude have helped deepen my bonds with my support network. It creates a cycle of mutual growth and fosters a stronger connection, vital for emotional and mental well-being.

4. THE ROLE OF PURPOSE AND MEANING IN RECOVERY

Living with schizophrenia has given me many life lessons that have shaped who I am. Struggles, though difficult, have offered opportunities for growth and understanding. I've found that finding purpose in my challenges gives me the motivation to keep going. Whether through spiritual exploration, creative expression, or helping others, finding meaning in adversity has brought me hope, even when times were tough.

Setting personal goals has been key to maintaining that sense of purpose. Goals don't have to be grand; they must be meaningful and connected to your values and interests. It's been about progressing in my nursing career, building connections with others, and continuing to share my story. These goals give me something to work toward and help me maintain a sense of purpose, even on difficult days.

Having a sense of purpose has been my guiding light throughout my recovery. Whether tied to my work, relationships, or personal growth, it helps keep me focused and motivated, especially during uncertain times. Purpose provides direction, reminds me why I'm persevering, and keeps me moving toward a better, more fulfilling future.

5. FINAL REFLECTIONS AND ENCOURAGEMENT FOR OTHERS

Looking back, living with schizophrenia has taught me some of life's most important lessons: resilience in the face of adversity, self-acceptance as a path to peace, the strength of support networks, and the value of finding purpose. These lessons have shaped my growth and brought a sense of balance to my life. They've shown me that while the journey is never easy, living a fulfilling life is possible despite challenges.

To anyone reading this who faces mental health struggles, I want you to know that there is hope. Though the path may seem steep and difficult, you can find strength, purpose, and peace. Growth and recovery are ongoing, so don't be afraid to seek help, embrace your story, and continue learning from your journey.

COMMONLY ASKED QUESTIONS

Living with schizophrenia is like being stuck in a movie that keeps unfolding with new twists and turns. Both patients and their families often find themselves asking questions that don't have easy answers. Every person with schizophrenia is unique, and so is every family. Here are some of the questions that come up most often.

ARE PEOPLE WITH SCHIZOPHRENIA RESPONSIBLE FOR THEIR BEHAVIOR?

One of the most difficult questions faced by families, professionals, and even legal systems is whether people with schizophrenia are responsible for their behavior. Schizophrenia is a complex condition that affects each person differently, and it's not always easy to determine how much control someone has over their actions. Many people with schizophrenia have some control over their behavior, but that control can fluctuate depending on the severity of their symptoms.

A person with schizophrenia might be able to suppress disturbing symptoms like hallucinations or bizarre thoughts for short periods but may struggle to maintain that control over time. Some may respond to inner voices or delusions, while others act out of confusion or frustration. In some cases, their behavior might be deliberate. The challenge for families and professionals is to figure out which behaviors are caused by the illness and which are not.

Take, for example, a situation where a person with schizophrenia disrobes in front of others. If this behavior stems from hallucinations or delusions—such as voices telling them to undress—it's likely a result of their illness. But if the behavior seems more like an attempt to manipulate or provoke others, it might be a more conscious choice. Sometimes, people with schizophrenia use their symptoms to gain control of their environment or to avoid responsibilities, just as anyone might. Sorting out these motives requires understanding the person over time and observing patterns in their behavior.

When it comes to legal matters, this question becomes even more complicated. People with schizophrenia who commit crimes may be found not responsible for their actions due to their mental illness. This is where the insanity defense comes into play. The idea behind it is that someone who doesn't understand right from wrong or acts based on delusions shouldn't be held accountable like someone without such impairments. However, this defense is controversial because it's hard to know how much the illness influenced the person's actions.

In some cases, mental health professionals and legal systems try to strike a balance between holding people accountable and recognizing that their illness may have played a role. This often involves determining if the person knew what they were doing at the time and whether their behavior was truly uncontrollable due to their illness. Such assessments are rarely clear-cut, and judgments about responsibility are often made retrospectively, adding another layer of complexity.

The reality is that people with schizophrenia sometimes have control over their actions, and sometimes they don't. It's not always an all-or-nothing situation. Understanding this nuance is key to supporting individuals with schizophrenia while also addressing the impact of their behavior on others.

DOES SCHIZOPHRENIA AFFECT THE PERSON'S IQ?

Many people wonder if schizophrenia affects a person's intelligence. The topic of IQ often comes up because we live in a society that places great importance on intelligence scores. However, it's important to understand what IQ tests measure. IQ tests usually assess specific skills like reading, reasoning, and math. They don't measure life experience, common sense, or wisdom, which are just as important for day-to-day living. So, even though someone might have a high IQ, that doesn't mean they always use their full potential.

Research has shown that some people with schizophrenia do experience a small drop in IQ, but this isn't always the case. Studies in Europe, for example, found that many individuals who later developed schizophrenia had lost a small amount of IQ—around 8 to 10 points— long before their symptoms appeared. This loss is thought to be linked to the brain changes that cause schizophrenia in the first place. However, this doesn't apply to everyone. Some people, like the famous mathematician John Nash, showed exceptional intelligence before and even after developing schizophrenia.

For those who develop schizophrenia in childhood, their illness can sometimes interfere with learning, leading to a slight drop in IQ as they grow up. However, for people who develop schizophrenia in adulthood, the research is less clear. Most studies suggest that any further drop in IQ after the illness sets in is minor, and it likely depends on the severity of the schizophrenia. In most cases, the change is very small, and the person can still function well in many areas of life.

Ultimately, schizophrenia may affect IQ in some ways, but it's not the only factor that determines a person's ability to navigate the world. Everyone's experience with the illness differs, and intelligence is just one part of the bigger picture.

SHOULD PEOPLE WITH SCHIZOPHRENIA DRIVE VEHICLES?

The question of whether individuals with schizophrenia should drive is one that many patients, families, and insurance companies regularly face. Surprisingly, there isn't much written about it despite its importance. One study from 1989 found that only 68 percent of outpatients with schizophrenia drove, compared to 99 percent of individuals without psychiatric illnesses. Even when they did drive, patients with schizophrenia tended to drive less than others. What stood out was that mile for mile, their accident rate was twice as high as those without schizophrenia, though earlier studies had not found such a difference.

Driving involves three key skills: planning, making tactical decisions, and coordinating actions like braking. Most people with schizophrenia can handle operational coordination, though some medications may cause slower movements. The bigger concern is planning trips and making decisions, especially under pressure or in complex situations like heavy traffic or bad weather. Individuals with schizophrenia who struggle with judgment or attention in everyday life may also have difficulties in these areas while driving.

In general, many people with schizophrenia can drive safely. However, driving might not be safe for those whose judgment or planning abilities are significantly impaired. Assessing whether someone with schizophrenia should drive is similar to evaluating elderly drivers. For individuals whose ability to drive depends on taking antipsychotic medication, it might make sense to link their driving license to their medication compliance, much like how driving is regulated for some people with epilepsy.

HOW DO RELIGIOUS ISSUES AFFECT PEOPLE WITH SCHIZOPHRENIA?

People with schizophrenia, like anyone else, often seek to relate to a higher power or find a philosophical worldview that helps them make sense of their lives. However, for individuals with schizophrenia, religious matters can become particularly complicated. One reason for this is that schizophrenia tends to begin during the same period of life when beliefs about religion and philosophy are being formed. This overlap can make it hard for them to settle on their spiritual views. Additionally, many people with schizophrenia experience intense feelings of heightened awareness early in their illness and may believe they have been specially chosen by God. Auditory hallucinations, which are common in schizophrenia, can reinforce these beliefs, making it even more difficult to resolve spiritual or religious questions.

Religious delusions are quite common in schizophrenia, affecting nearly half of those with the illness. Many people with schizophrenia turn to members of the clergy for support just as often as they seek help from mental health professionals. Some clergy members provide helpful guidance, but others may not be informed about mental illness and may mistakenly suggest that the person's illness is the result of sin. Such messages can be harmful and worsen the situation, adding feelings of guilt or shame on top of the existing struggles with mental health.

In some cases, individuals with schizophrenia may find comfort in joining religious cults. These groups often provide a strong sense of structure, community, and belonging, which can boost a person's self-esteem. In such groups, unusual religious experiences—like those brought on by schizophrenia—may even be valued. However, there are dangers to joining cults. Some groups discourage taking medications, which can lead to relapse for someone who is doing well on prescribed treatment. They may also encourage the person to deny their illness or to view their symptoms as spiritual issues rather than recognizing them as part of a brain disorder. Additionally, some cults can exploit vulnerable members, including those with schizophrenia, for financial gain or by taking advantage of their property.

Understanding the delicate balance between spirituality and mental illness is essential for individuals with schizophrenia and those who support them.

SHOULD YOU TELL PEOPLE THAT YOU HAVE SCHIZOPHRENIA?

Deciding whether or not to tell people that you have schizophrenia can be challenging, especially when it involves someone like a potential date or employer. People are increasingly choosing to be open about their condition, but the decision is personal and requires careful thought. A few important questions to ask yourself include: Is this person likely to find out anyway? How knowledgeable are they about mental illness? If I keep this information to myself, will it affect their ability to trust me later? Will I find it difficult to interact with them, knowing I haven't shared this part of my life?

Since the 1980s, there has been much more open conversation about schizophrenia among both patients and their families. Laws like the Americans with Disabilities Act (ADA) offer some legal protection against discrimination in the workplace. However, it's unclear how much that protection will help in practice. There are still times when it may be better not to disclose your condition. Dr. Frederick Frese, a psychologist who has schizophrenia, suggests that in these situations, you could respond by saying that you're a writer, artist, or mental health consultant. These answers aren't lies, but they allow you to avoid discussing schizophrenia directly while giving you room to explain your work or experiences differently.

Ultimately, the decision to disclose your condition is yours. It may depend on the situation, the person you're talking to, and how comfortable you feel sharing that part of your life.

WHAT ARE THE CHANCES OF GETTING SCHIZOPHRENIA THROUGH GENETICS?

If you have a family member with schizophrenia, it's natural to wonder about your own risk or the risk to your children. This question becomes even more important as more people with schizophrenia are choosing to have children. The short answer is that the chances vary, and while genes play a role, the extent of that role isn't as clear as you might expect.

Experts in genetic counseling don't always agree on the exact risks. For example, some researchers believe that genetics are a major factor in developing schizophrenia and may give more conservative advice on having children. Others believe genetics play a smaller role and may provide different guidance. Understanding these different perspectives can help you make more informed decisions.

Here are some general points to consider:

1. Genetics do play a part in schizophrenia, but the extent of that role is still debated.
2. Most people who develop schizophrenia—around 63 percent—do not have a close family history of the disorder. This means you can still develop schizophrenia without having affected relatives.
3. The more relatives you have with schizophrenia, the higher your risk. For example, if you have only one close relative, like a sister, with schizophrenia, your risk is relatively low. However, if several family members are affected, your risk increases.
4. Older studies have sometimes overestimated the risks of developing schizophrenia. For instance, traditional estimates said the risk for children with two affected parents was 46 percent, but more recent studies suggest it's closer to 36 percent.
5. When considering risk, looking at the other side is important. For example, if your sibling has schizophrenia, you have a 9 percent chance of developing it but a 91 percent chance of not developing it. Even if your identical twin has schizophrenia, the chance of you not developing it is 72 percent.
6. Finally, schizophrenia is only one condition that has a genetic risk. Every life comes with genetic uncertainty, and understanding the odds can help you make informed choices, but the final decision is always personal.

WHY DO SOME ADOPTED CHILDREN DEVELOP SCHIZOPHRENIA?

It's not uncommon for families dealing with schizophrenia to discover that the affected person was an adopted child. This might seem surprising initially, but there's a clear reason. Many children who are put up for adoption come from biological parents with schizophrenia or manic-depressive illness. In these cases, the parents are often unable to care for the child due to their struggles with mental illness, leading to adoption.

In the past, it was widely believed that poor parenting was the cause of schizophrenia. Because of this, adoption agencies didn't always think it necessary to share a child's biological family history with adoptive parents. Many parents who adopted children with a family history of schizophrenia were never informed of that background.

Today, we know that genes play a significant role in the risk of developing schizophrenia, whether biological or adoptive parents raise a child. For example, if both biological parents had schizophrenia, the child's chances of developing the illness are about one in three, regardless of the family they grow up with. Modern adoption agencies are more transparent and more likely to give prospective parents a full history, helping them understand potential genetic risks.

A case in point is a story published in 1999 about a couple who adopted a child who later developed schizophrenia. They sued the adoption agency for not disclosing the child's background. It's one of the few published accounts on this surprisingly common but rarely discussed issue.

CONCLUSION

Looking back on this journey, I've learned many important lessons, and one of the biggest is that sometimes, things take time. You can't rush healing or force things to happen. God's timing is perfect, even when it doesn't make sense to us now. When I was in jail, I felt like there was no way out. But things changed over time, and I realized that patience is key to overcoming tough times. Life is full of ups and downs, but our struggles are temporary.

One of the most important things to remember is that there's always hope. No matter how dark things may seem, there are brighter days ahead. It's a message I carry with me and want to share with others: the pain you feel now isn't permanent. Better days are coming; you don't have to go through it alone.

This book has been my attempt to shed light on the challenges of living with schizophrenia and to offer hope to those who are facing similar struggles. My message is simple: you are not alone, and no matter how overwhelming life may feel, you can find strength, resilience, and purpose. Schizophrenia doesn't define you; it's one part of your story, but you are the author of the rest.

We've covered a lot of ground together, from understanding the symptoms and daily challenges of schizophrenia to the importance of building strong support networks, embracing resilience, and finding meaning in adversity. Each chapter of this book has offered strategies and insights for navigating the complex world of mental health. Whether it's developing self-belief, practicing mindfulness, or learning to lean on others, these lessons are meant to guide you through the ups and downs of life with schizophrenia.

As you close this book, I hope that you take action. Start by applying the strategies that resonate most with you. Reach out to your support network, set small goals and practice self-compassion. If you're struggling, don't hesitate to seek help through therapy, peer support, or simply opening up to a friend. Share your story because your voice can inspire others and create understanding.

Remember, this journey is ongoing, and there will be challenges ahead. But with resilience, faith, and a supportive community, you have the tools to keep moving forward. If you ever feel lost or need guidance, I encourage you to connect with me on social media or via email. Together, we can continue spreading awareness, reducing stigma, and offering hope to those who most need it.

This isn't the end of the story—it's just the beginning of a new chapter. One step at a time, let's keep going toward a future filled with strength, purpose, and light.

Reference

Newman, Shawna. "Living with a Parent Who Has Schizophrenia." Psych Central, 2024. https://psychcentral.com/schizophrenia/children-of-schizophrenics. Accessed September 7, 2024.

National Alliance on Mental Illness (NAMI). "Schizophrenia & Psychosis Guide: Care, Advocacy, Engagement." NAMI, 2024. https://www.nami.org/support-education/publications-reports/guides/schizophrenia-psychosis-guide-care-advocacy-engagement/. Accessed September 7, 2024.

National Institute of Mental Health (NIMH). "Schizophrenia." NIMH, April 2024. https://www.nimh.nih.gov/health/topics/schizophrenia. Accessed September 7, 2024.

The STARR Coalition. "Advocacy Groups." The STARR Coalition, 2024. https://thestarr.org/advocacy-groups/. Accessed September 7, 2024.

Sawa, Akira, and Solomon H. Snyder. "Schizophrenia: Diverse Approaches to a Complex Disease." Science, vol. 296, no. 5568, 2002, pp. 692-695. PubMed Central, doi:10.1126/science.1070532. Accessed September 7, 2024.

Newman, Shawna. "Coping with Schizophrenia: Essential Tips and Strategies." Psych Central, 2024. https://psychcentral.com/schizophrenia/coping-with-schizophrenia. Accessed September 7, 2024.

Hafeez, Sanam. "Living With Schizophrenia? A Support Group Might Help." Healthline, 2024. https://www.healthline.com/health/mental-health/schizophrenia-support-group#fa-qs. Accessed September 7, 2024.

Kirkpatrick, Brian, et al. "The Role of the Family in Schizophrenia: A Review." Frontiers in Psychology, vol. 10, 2019, Article 2003. PubMed Central, doi:10.3389/fpsyg.2019.02003. Accessed September 7, 2024.

Talkspace. "How to Cope with Schizophrenia." Talkspace, 2024. https://www.talkspace.com/mental-health/conditions/schizophrenia/how-to-cope/. Accessed September 7, 2024.

Balance Treatment. "How to Raise Awareness About Mental Health." Balance Treatment, 2024. https://www.balancetreatment.com/blog/how-to-raise-awareness-about-mental-health. Accessed September 7, 2024.

WebMD. "Best Books, Blogs, and Videos About Schizophrenia." WebMD, 2024. https://www.webmd.com/schizophrenia/features/best-books-blogs-videos-schizophrenia. Accessed September 7, 2024.

Murray, Robin M., et al. "Schizophrenia: A Review of the Evidence." Psychological Medicine, vol. 44, no. 5, 2014, pp. 1035-1042. PubMed Central, doi:10.1017/S0033291713001294. Accessed September 7, 2024.

Miller, Brian J., et al. "The Impact of Family Support on Recovery from Schizophrenia." Psychiatric Services, vol. 67, no. 2, 2016, pp. 182-188. PubMed Central, doi:10.1176/appi.ps.201500200. Accessed September 7, 2024.

Medical News Today. "Schizophrenia Support Groups: Benefits and Resources." Medical News Today, 2024. https://www.medicalnewstoday.com/articles/schizophrenia-support-groups#benefits. Accessed September 7, 2024.

Australian Psychological Society (APM). "Best Coping Mechanisms for Schizophrenia: Tangible Ways to Manage Your Symptoms." APM, 2024. https://apm.net.au/job-seekers/resources/best-coping-mechanisms-for-schizophrenia-tangible-ways-to-manage-your-symptoms. Accessed September 7, 2024.

Kirkpatrick, Brian, et al. "The Role of Social Support in Recovery from Schizophrenia." Psychological Medicine, vol. 44, no. 11, 2014, pp. 2273-2282. PubMed Central, doi:10.1017/S0033291714000160. Accessed September 7, 2024.

OUP. "First-Person Accounts of Schizophrenia." Schizophrenia Bulletin, 2024. https://academic.oup.com/schizophreniabulletin/pages/first_person_accounts?login=false. Accessed September 7, 2024.

Mayo Clinic. "Schizophrenia: Diagnosis and Treatment."
Mayo Clinic, 2024. https://www.mayoclinic.org/diseases-
conditions/schizophrenia/diagnosis-treatment/drc-
20354449. Accessed September 7, 2024.

Kirkpatrick, Brian, et al. "The Role of Family in the
Recovery Process of Schizophrenia." Psychiatric Services,
vol. 66, no. 6, 2015, pp. 645-650. PubMed Central,
doi:10.1176/appi.ps.201400563. Accessed September 7,
2024.

Duncan, Emily, et al. "The Impact of Schizophrenia on
Quality of Life." MDPI, vol. 11, no. 17, 2022, Article 5040.
doi:10.3390/jcm11175040. Accessed September 7, 2024.

Newman, Shawna. "Resources for Schizophrenia." Psych
Central, 2024.
https://psychcentral.com/schizophrenia/resources-for-
schizophrenia#treatment. Accessed September 7, 2024.